AUTISM-ASPERGER'S
& sexuality

PUBERTY AND BEYOND

JERRY AND MARY NEWPORT

Foreword by Teresa Bolick, Ph.D.

FUTURE HORIZONS INC.

AUTISM, ASPERGER'S & SEXUALITY
All marketing and publishing rights guaranteed to and reserved by

FUTURE HORIZONS INC.

721 W. Abram Street
Arlington, Texas 76013
800-489-0727
817-277-0727
817-277-2270 (fax)
www.FHautism.com
E-mail: info@FHautism.com

ISBN 10: 1-885477-88-0
ISBN 13: 978-1-885477-88-0

Table of Contents

The Autism and Asperger's Syndrome Independent Living Association recognizes and affirms that individuals with Autism and Asperger's Syndrome are people with sexual feelings, needs and identities, and believes that sexuality should always be seen in the total context of human relationships. Sexuality includes gender identity, friendships, self-esteem, body image and awareness, emotional development and social behavior, as well as involvement in physical expressions of love, affection and desires.

FOREWORD

by Dr. Teresa Bolick, author of *Asperger's and Adolescence*

Jerry Newport has dared to go where no man (or woman) went before. In collaboration with his wife Mary, he tackles dating, relationships, and sexuality issues for individuals with Asperger's Syndrome (AS) and autism. With the same direct and humorous style used in *Your Life Is Not a Label*, Jerry and Mary provide information and advice that warrants the attention of adolescents and young adults with or without AS.

In an era when "valuing differences" and "political correctness" are often the norm, Jerry and Mary give the lowdown on getting to know others. They are candid about the real reactions of many people. They provide concrete and specific advice about hygiene and appearance. Their initial message is, "Even if you don't care how you look, smell, etc., others will." Practical advice ranges from how to shave with minimal skin irritation to how to buy decent clothing on a tight budget. Jerry and Mary present a balance between encouraging behavior that others will find appealing and discouraging behavior that others will find "fake."

Throughout the book, Jerry and Mary emphasize the importance of self-confidence and practice. They encourage "dry runs" of everything from smiling to managing the transportation on a date.

The message, "You can relax more easily if you know what's happening," echoes through each chapter. The corollary, "Others will be more comfortable if you're relaxed," is illustrated as well. They truly believe (and teach) that anyone can do the "relationship thing" with sufficient information, planning, and interest. Many adolescents with AS and other social communication challenges struggle with the "unwritten rules" of meeting, greeting, dating, and beyond.

Jerry and Mary provide a translation of much of the social behavior that baffles individuals with AS. They even answer many of the unasked questions, questions that never occurred to many of us. They teach "rules of thumb" for interpreting the contradictory social behavior that is rampant in modern society. When does "maybe" mean, "Ask me another time," and when does it mean "no?" Was Grandma right when she said, "Beauty is only skin deep?" With this "guidebook," the reader is infinitely better equipped to enter the all-too-confusing world of romantic relationships.

Past "clinical wisdom" assumed that individuals with AS or autism weren't interested in relationships. Well, remember that old joke about what happens when we assume. (If you don't know the answer, ask one of your "jock" friends.) It's probably true that some people with AS aren't interested in romantic or close relationships. (It's definitely true that some people without AS aren't interested in romantic or close relationships!) But it's also true that you don't know if you like chocolate until you taste it. Too many folks with AS or autism haven't had the chance to find out if they "like chocolate" because they haven't had the opportunity to "taste" relationships. Until recently, most education or intervention programs skipped over the relationship piece, preferring to concentrate instead on the neater world of English grammar and algebra. Most programs certainly didn't teach students to take a chance on relationships. Jerry and Mary encourage the process of "tasting" and recommend strategies to make the most of opportunities that do come along. They also provide lots of reassurance for times when things go wrong. In the end, it's a personal choice whether or not to pursue romance and relationships. But we do want to make sure that a person has the skills if he or she decides to "taste" the relationship world. Jerry and Mary outline a series of steps to develop and support these skills.

In a culture where "sex sells," it's tough for many adolescents and adults to understand that intimacy is first and foremost about the relationship. Jerry and Mary wade boldly into this complicated area, guiding without preaching and translating without trivializing. Much of their wisdom should be "required reading" for any adolescent or young adult. Jerry and Mary remind us to be caring and feeling beings, not just sexual creatures.

Against the background of intimacy and relationships, Jerry and Mary confront the nitty-gritty of sexuality. With characteristic candor, they talk about what sexual contact may feel like for both of the parties. They provide practical and specific "do's and don'ts." And they do it with enough humor to remind us that life and love are supposed to be fun.

This book isn't just for folks with AS, autism, or other social communication glitches, though. It's for all of us. It reminded me of the assumptions (that word again!) that "neurotypicals" and other "normal" people make about what is "normal" and what is "disabled." It also reminded me of a National Public Radio interview with a well-known author. After losing the use of his legs in an accident, the author was asked what it felt like to be disabled. He replied, "I don't think of myself as disabled. I think of the rest of you as 'temporarily abled.'" I often reflect upon these words when faced with the social "goofs" made by me and those around me. There's always something that each of us botches or something we can't do "in the moment." It doesn't take having AS or autism to make it important to learn and practice social skills and closeness. In this warm, funny and helpful book, Jerry and Mary acknowledge the imperfections of all of us (including people with AS) but go on to teach, cajole, encourage, and entertain. They leave us with messages about AS and autism but, most importantly, with messages about being human.

Teresa Bolick, PH.D.

Message From the Editor

This book is offered to assist individuals on the autism/Asperger's spectrum, their parents and caregivers, in the important areas of sociality and sexual interest.

We chose Jerry and Mary Newport, a married couple, to write this book. They were chosen because they are both on the spectrum. In this way, the book would have a view from "inside the puzzle," rather than that of a professional who would view it much more dispassionately. Their perspectives are unique and reflect their experiences, recommendations and advice to those who follow them into the social and sexual world.

We are confident that they have brought valuable information that will be very helpful to many.

This was a very difficult subject to edit and caused more than one "in-depth" conversation in our office over what to leave in and what to delete. In the final analysis, I made the decisions as to the final form of the book.

However, as a father of two neurotypical young ladies and a man with autism, I am very sensitive to my responsibility in reviewing the information they should receive. This sensitivity leads me to understand that there are sections that may not be appropriate for some, particularly younger people on the spectrum. However, there are many other chapters that may be very important at certain stages of their development. Therefore, I am making a special exception to the copyright policy of Future Horizons for this book.

Any parent or caregiver is authorized to copy any five chapters of this book to give to an individual without getting prior approval from our office. (Obviously, this policy is for only this Future Horizons book.) In this way, a caregiver can choose what, and when, information should be read. We certainly hope this policy will enable you to maximize the effectiveness of the advice and information in this book.

Sincerely,

R. Wayne Gilpin

President, Future Horizons, Inc.

Authors' Introduction

We are a married couple with autism/Asperger's Syndrome. That unique fact is the main reason Future Horizons asked us to write this book. The President explained that we could offer an entirely different view of the sexual world because of our experiences and place in life now. It is true that we have not only seen the abuse, rejection and confusion endured by those on the spectrum, we have lived it.

In considering the offer to write this book, we still wondered if we were the ones to do the job. After all, isn't a book like this the responsibility of professionals? But as we read what was available, we quickly realized that if anyone can convince our peers and those who love us that sexuality is an appropriate and necessary part of autistic life and education, it must be our people who do it. It is our sincere hope that this "different" perspective brings new knowledge to the reader.

The "sexual explosion" hits all of us. The realization that boys and girls really are different and that there is a reason why, is a huge and often traumatic event for our people, with lifetime implications. It may be the most difficult issue for many families. My parents were wonderful in many ways. However, sex was, of all topics, the one that my family just never discussed. That omission was unusual since my father, two brothers and my mom engaged in discussions/arguments over everything else. Meals were verbal food fights on a daily basis.

But there was no room for talking about sex. It was similar for Mary. Without question, we both feel that we would have been much better prepared to meet the complexity of relationships had we had discussions with our parents on this subject.

That is why Mary and I wrote this book. We understand that this is a very important stage in life. We remember the initial desire, rejection, alienation and all that came with it. We know from our own experience, from what many adult peers have shared, and what we see in adolescents and young adults today. My partner and I hope that this book will help our young peers and the important people in their lives to understand, discuss, and develop realistic expectations and lifelong coping strategies in response to that event that hits us all in life. **And it hits a lot sooner today than it did in the sixties!**

As we said, this book is by two authors. You will always be able to tell who is writing in this way: *Italics will indicate passages written by Mary Newport*. The rest will be by me, Jerry Newport. We felt that we had to write this in a "realistic" manner. To that end, all pretenses had to be discarded as we discussed sex. In doing so, we will reveal aspects of our past that we have not discussed publicly before. We believe that two rational, objective, sincere people, who are both proudly "on the spectrum," can make a contribution to general understanding of this important subject.

We have interviewed many individuals on the spectrum, but we will obviously protect the privacy of those who have shared their experiences. Real names are not used unless they have already appeared in a widely read publication, such as a personal account or a letter to a newsletter of an autism organization. In order to further protect privacy, specific geographic locations are avoided. "Urban" or words like "midwestern" are as close as we will get.

For example, in a supportive peer group setting, a teenager, "John," shares his obsession with a pretty female teenage peer. She does not share his feelings. John is depressed. He announces that he is thinking of committing suicide because of how he feels. (Note: Most in that meeting felt that the threat was a plea for help and not an actual plan. However, all discussions on this subject must be taken seriously. Too many pleas like this are not responded to properly, and the result is a disaster that no one truly wants to happen.) In this case, after counseling and assistance, John didn't act on his pain and he is alive and well. Today he is a much older, wiser, flexible, and independent young man who is living a good life. But it took a lot of great people to help him get there. That is the good news.

The bad news is this: The desire for a girlfriend, which often goes along with a sex drive, was so important to this young man that his failure made him wonder whether life was worth living. How far out of line is this? We wonder. Even "normal" people blow up and do crazy things to themselves and others because of breakups in relationships or other rejections. So why would it be any different for people who are already pushed near the breaking point by a lifetime of rejection and inferiority?

This example is much closer to home: A fifth grade Asperger's girl is in bloom. She is pretty, awakening to sexual interest, but socially clueless. An adult man, a neighbor, initiates her into the sexual arena. This went on for three years until, at age 14, the secret came out. Her family was embarrassed and didn't act in a supportive way at all. They felt that the embarrassment had to be covered up. The solution was to allow the girl to join a traveling religious group and just go anywhere as long as the family could avoid the issue. Out-of-sight, out-of-mind and out-to-lunch. That was Mary, now my wife, in 1970.

Her "sin" was to want something that everyone else seemed to want. Additionally, she was gaining approval from people she trusted by indulging in sex with them. Obviously, if anyone sinned in that case, it was the people around her who valued their public image and their legal security more than her welfare.

The miracle is that Mary survived all that and other insults to become the fine mother, professional and advocate that she is today.

This subject can't be examined without considering media, school and other influences. These shape the way that all kids, including ours, look at their world. But this book cannot expand its scope to cover all of those influences as deeply as we would like as we strive to understand our primary subject. That is left to other writers.

We will present a narrative on the sexual awakening in our population and its impact as we become adults. Next comes a likely scenario for how our children survive the initial introduction of sexual awareness in their lives. That will be followed by a discussion of what parents should say to their newly sexually aware children, as well as when and how to say it. The parental part of the equation is not a one shot deal and must become a permanent, accepted part of family dialogue.

That discussion is followed by survival strategies, dating advice, and other social dynamics. We share as many coping strategies and positives as we can, but we can't be a Pollyanna about this. For many of our peers, sexual awakening is a huge nightmare, the biggest one of their young lives.

We deal with social responsibility: birth control, hygiene and disease prevention. We offer our views on the responsibilities of sexual activity. We also recognize that not every one will choose a conventional form of sexuality or necessarily, any sexuality.

The "Roads Less Traveled" chapter, near the end, aims to recognize and support individual rights of sexual and social lifestyle choices.

Finally, we offer long-term perspectives on sex, its changing significance in one's life and constructive strategies to help people from our community grow socially and sexually at any stage of life, from puberty to adulthood.

In conclusion, Mary and I thank you for giving us a chance to share our ideas and feelings and hope they prove helpful to those on the spectrum, their loved ones, and caregivers.

We thank the rest of you for just being there.

Mary Newport and Jerry Newport

Tucson, AZ.

Social or Sexual Relationships are not Created Overnight

The feelings of sexual desire don't happen overnight. Gradual steps lead an adolescent to that day. There is a subtle escalation of contact and awareness that takes years from the first time that age peers of both genders meet. It is an important developmental dance for all youth. It is a dance most autistic children don't even notice until it has been obvious to everyone else for a long time. Then, they want to dance, but they will have missed out on years of pre-dance classes.

The evidence of early autistic development supports the above. Our children are most often taken in for evaluation because they don't respond to their surrounding world as normal children do. The most frequent hope is that the child may have a hearing problem. How else to explain the child who doesn't respond to your voice, the child who doesn't want to play normally, interact with his siblings and who would rather sit by himself, rock, etc.

The good news is that more of our children grow out of their initial self-absorption enough to begin talking and doing other essential tasks. Many of them learn what is called "experience sharing" in *Solving the Relationship Puzzle* by Dr. Stephen Gutstein. What is even more important is what most of these improved youths have still not learned. That is what my friend, Dr. Gutstein, calls "the ability to dance." This is the ability to do things of a spontaneous nature with other people. These are things that the person cannot do alone. These require the youth to have a relationship with another person.

That is totally different from necessary, individual skills that many of our autistic children can learn from ABA, Greenspan, TEAACH and other approaches. These are all good steps in the right direction. It is logical for them to learn those, like brushing teeth, putting on clothes, learning other basics, because the activity is not complicated by dependency on the presence of another person.

However, these skills are still a far cry from a child who is confident, flexible and integrated with his peers in every activity. Social pre-school, if you wish to call it that, requires development beyond doing something for a reward or by oneself. It involves doing things for enjoyment with other people because one wants to do that activity and wants to share it with someone, not just anyone but a special someone in a pattern of mutual experience sharing.

There are years of playing in the sandbox, playground and other activities in which our children do not participate very well. The importance of these activities cannot be overestimated. This is the training ground for social activity in the teenage and adult years. Early social intervention and training is important to lay the groundwork for future social activity.

Some eventually function well enough to go to school in a reasonably independent manner and might even stand still and smile for a class photo. In that sense, "they look just like the others." But in the ways that count to peers, they are not seen that way. We have made a lot of progress, but there is much more ground our educators must cover to teach early social skills to help our children have a happy and integrated childhood.

Many children progress far enough to function well in a regular classroom without an aide. Obviously, there are many benefits to having an aide assist one of our kids. However, it is important to remember the social downside of an aide. When an aide is present, it is a clear signal to the child's peers. Imagine yourself in a class with any student who has an aide adult attached to him like Velcro™. You would think, "What is wrong with that kid?" He may be the last person you will want to have as a "best pal."

It is just a different reaction when an aide is for a person with autism. The child doesn't look like he has a problem. Other children with aides have physical or developmental conditions that are visually obvious. The aide just reinforces that truth and may even make the student a sympathetic character. That was the case with a student with spina bifida, a fourth grader I met while running an elementary school library. He had friends and was very well liked. His aide was also liked by the students and helped them in class when he could. His disability was obvious and drew sympathy and interest from the other students.

Many autistic children get no such slack when seen with an aide in a normal classroom because they often don't look like they should need assistance. This presents a dilemma for any parent who sees benefits in mainstreamed educational settings. One has to weigh the benefits perceived against the stigma of the aide. Question: Is the inclusion for the child or for the parent's ego, so he can say, "My child is fine now. He's in a regular class just like yours." But the truth may be that if this was really true, he may not need an aide. However, it should be emphasized that this is a case-by-case basis. Parents have to look inside and estimate what is best for their child. Many times inclusion with an aide is very beneficial to the child and can be for the other students, if the inclusion is handled with sensitivity. In Sheila Wagner's book, *Inclusive Programming for Elementary Students with Autism,* she lays out plans that have been effective for all concerned.

Attitudes of young students can be changed, but it takes special effort. Some of my peers have gone into elementary schools and talked to students about what it was like to grow up with autism, to have such a real yet "invisible" condition. A smart ASA chapter or Asperger's group can make sure that local schools have biographical material from autistic people, to go along with the standard books about Helen Keller, etc. But most children, unfortunately, aren't being exposed to this and to them, an aide may mean, "Stay away from this student!"

In a more restrictive environment, the aide may not inspire the same reaction because other students may share the same aide or a similar person. But the restrictive environment may have negative aspects. It may be a class, mainly for SED children, "Severely Emotionally Disturbed," a frequent dumping ground for our children. This could be the case of bringing the natural victim to the natural abuser.

Inclusion is complicated. I know professionals such as Ms. Wagner who have devoted their careers to understanding it, so I won't insult them by claiming to sum it all up here. This much, I know: there is certainly no one method that works for all our children. But it is foolish to ignore the social impact of being in normal settings with an adult aide. I believe the best form of inclusion is probably one that starts in activities where the student can enjoy himself and participate without the aide or at least with the hope of fading an aide out of the picture.

The more a child is seen in school, without an aide attached, the better his eventual social image. Remember too, that even if fading of the aide is the eventual goal of the parents and administrators, that aide may not wish to have to think about another assignment. An "easy child," one who really doesn't need you any more or only minimally, makes for an easier day than a new assignment. That same perception applies throughout life with any support staff. I believe that some aides can and will, encourage dependency on themselves, not in the child's interest, but for their own job security. Don't always assume that people working with your child have his or her interests in mind. Everyone has an agenda.

With or without aides, there are places where you can easily identify autistic children: any place where the usual activity is unstructured, like the playground. Some of our kids will thrive or at least pass in the classroom, but games are something else. You can find them on the outskirts, perfect targets for apprentice bullies. The playground is also where kidding, teasing and other contact games begin between the genders. Again, special effort must be made with our kids during this "social training ground."

Many of our kids are way too enclosed in an over-stimulated bubble to even notice what they are missing. Parents and teachers should recognize how important it is at this point to involve them as much as the child can handle. It is often easy to let them stay in their own little world, because it is extra work to encourage involvement.

I first noticed this much later, while employed at Grant Elementary School in the spring of 1987. The school was in Santa Monica. It had an interesting mix of cultures. There were six levels: kindergarten through grade five. At the older end, I had to keep middle school boys from sneaking onto the property to "hit on" fifth grade girls who were already taller and sometimes, more developed than many mothers.

In the hallways, some fifth graders tried to get away with holding hands, much as high school students did in my generation. One recess, a bunch of them came into a library. The group all clustered around a couple, sitting as far away from me as possible. They all waited until finally, the boy kissed the girl. They ran giggling out of the library.

Five-year-olds weren't nearly as advanced, but you could see some interaction even when they innocently walked to lunch or to the library. What was also noticeable was how some kids were so totally self-absorbed that they took part in none of this. There was only one boy in the school officially diagnosed with autism, but out of the four hundred there were others who today may be diagnosed as being on the spectrum. They usually stared anywhere but at another person. One kindergartner loved to read, already better than most of the school. He sat in the middle of the library with a science book and read it as his class got up and walked past him, back to class. He was very good at one thing at a time, but could blow up emotionally in a heartbeat. No diagnosis for him and others who should have been diagnosed and helped. But that was 1987, not now.

In between the youngest and oldest children, I noticed a spectrum of increased interest between boys and girls. Just as in my youth, girls seemed to develop this faster. They were often bigger than male classmates. It wasn't unusual to see girls teasing boys and even chasing them into my library or in the hallway. No real interaction at all but it is all the necessary kind of escalation that prepares kids for it.

It was an eye-opener to see before me what I had totally missed three decades before! I was far less autistic at that age than most who are diagnosed, even less so than most who have Asperger's Syndrome. Even I never took part in any of the preteen social activities that my peers did, although it was less advanced than for students in the eighties and far, far less forward than the kids of today.

So, it is easy to see that, without intensive social training at the younger ages, our kids are not ready for the suddenly increased social interactions of the puberty period.

The simple fact is that our children are ill-prepared when sexual awareness finally arrives. There is a shocking disappearance of a happy illusion he/she has of his place in school society before puberty. With proper intervention, many of them may be included in normal classes by the time puberty happens. In many ways, they feel much better about themselves, more secure and more hopeful about life in general than they did at two or three, when their differences led to the diagnosis.

However, even in the happiest of situations, whether it be mine, or Mary's, or many on record, our elementary school students still have a problem with self-image because no matter how good the report cards are, they already know that in the spontaneous sea of school life, they are still far behind.

One of the biggest differences is that most normal children have at least one special friend. The lack of even one friend is a common concern, across the board and especially in elementary school. I can't deal with how to improve this situation here. That is covered in books you will find in the appendix.

Some parents encourage the social activity at these early ages by bringing over "friends" for swim parties, TV watching groups or any social functions they can create. They find that their child does not interact normally, but many believe that there is some "osmosis" social education going on that benefit the child later in life.

However, it is not a good idea for parents or teachers to force social activities upon any child until he shows interest in school, neighborhood, activities, etc. If he shows even mild interest, increase the "dosage." You will probably be the most successful if you find a hobby or interest of his. Even if it means a parent sitting down with your son or daughter and a friend or two as you discuss *Dragon Ball Z* or anime (Heaven help you), the latest computer games, pro wrestling, dinosaur species, etc. It is important to your youngster and will help them to understand social skills as they model some of your behavior. It can be fun, and you will enjoy your time with your son or daughter.

Many autistic people, even as adults, do not express any natural desire to have friends as conventionally defined; people with whom you share secrets and have intimate contact. However, most of them do see some value in an intermediate relationship, that of an associate. An associate is someone who helps you perform an activity. This is someone you can trust long enough to complete that activity, but not necessarily someone who you even know by name. This may be someone, because of their official, recognized position, that can be trusted, at least within the parameters of the defined activity.

Now, look at the child's pre-puberty situation this way. All children have associates and acquaintances. An acquaintance may be someone who he or she has minimal contact with, but will occasionally show up in his life, a school bus driver or cafeteria worker may fall in this category. Most children have associates, acquaintances and friends. Your autistic child may regard his parents and siblings as associates at first. He certainly regards his teachers, aides, custodians and other people, who are a constant reliable and practical part of the school landscape, as associates.

Mary woke me up about this when I reflected on my youth. What I thought were friends were mostly like associates. To this day, Mary, other than me, prefers the relatively safety of knowing people for specific, defined reasons, like employers or tax-preparers. She uses association with them as long as they are reliable, trustworthy and help her do something necessary that she can't do alone. But that is as far as she wants it to go with most people. There is still no natural need to bond or feel intimacy with lots of friends. I guess that makes me the lucky exception!

But Mary seems to have enough of what she wants out of other people. If that is true, it seems that other autistic people can grow up to find a similar balance. Associate relationships that form early in life, for all children, with official people, give a clue as to how some classmates can eventually become associates, too.

It is important to accept these associate relationships as being as close to a friendship as people with autism are comfortable having in youth.

With autism, a pronounced adolescent preference for associates does not always change later, with the exception of a sole intimate partner. Maybe what needs to change is our obsession with getting all autistic children to have friends. In fact, many autistic adults who find partners report that those partners entered their life as trusted associates, people who could be relied on to share a necessary or even enjoyable activity. The difference is that these autistic adults were more ready to let down defenses, give up control and seek friendships and intimacy because they were less threatened by the world than they were as children. The best news about all associates is that the child is learning to seek reliability and trust as required attributes. That should carry over into any eventual friends or partner relationship.

The pre-puberty autistic youth is rarely as secure as he may seem. Remember, along with this sexual explosion, he or she is probably also managing the sensory stimulations and other challenges that led to his or her diagnosis. But managing means that you are still walking on eggs most of the time, a very exhausting experience though less stressful than knowing where the eggs are and how to detour around them. This constant state of "stop the world, I want to get off" anxiety is a big barrier to letting go of feelings, accepting and giving affection and all of the other things that friendships require. It makes the associate relationships more attractive. They are safer.

One good thing to include in school activity, at any level, is daily exercise. Team sports are usually confusing, but adaptive P.E. can be productive. There are many individual activities that can be done to maintain and improve fitness, even in children who have difficulty developing muscle tone (hypotonia). Put it this way, a child who is physically fit has better focus and self-esteem. He is also less likely to be an eventual playground target. It is enough of a challenge to have special needs without looking like a wimp.

I used to think that social conventions favor autistic girls in youth. Mary has educated me on this. Young girls with autism may acquire more sexual experience, but it is not necessarily positive. Sex in the form of abuse causes long-term damage. It also is not a social activity. The ideal is to grow socially and sexually. That happens for neither autistic gender, usually.

What makes it even harder for today's autistic children is that sexual awareness develops at an earlier age. The autistic child's illusion of quasi-acceptance is broken earlier. He has had less of a chance to work out even half of a truce with the school environment before puberty casts the final, insulting spotlight on his perceived inferiority.

I can only speak as a male. Most of us will be left out because we lack the assertiveness necessary for social initiation. Our self-consciousness and awkwardness sends out nonverbal warnings long before we even open our mouths. This happens whether we work up the courage to talk to a girl in the school hallway or stumble across the dance floor, en-route to a public rejection at a school dance, by someone who may not dance either but would rather be shot than be seen dancing with any of us!

The first wave is different for autistic girls but Mary can tell you about that much better.

Puberty helped in some respects because I became sexy. I did everything to cultivate my looks. My peers' reactions began to change in the ninth grade. I was not ridiculed as much. However, puberty was hard because adults were having sex with me, offering me marijuana, etc. I only had relationships with adults. None of my friends were my age.

My "popularity" was an illusion, and became one of the saddest parts of my life.

Both genders suffer initially. It may seem that autistic girls fare better if one only measures by sexual experience, regardless of how it is gained. However, a healthy model of social and sexual growth is not usually mirrored by either gender. If you have an autistic daughter with a "boyfriend," watch for signs of exploitation. What appears to be adolescent social development can be abuse instead of growth. The end can send your daughter backwards, not forwards.

If you have a typical autistic "wallflower" son, you can't assume that once in college, he will automatically become a "late bloomer" socially (see Late Bloomers - page 145). The earlier he begins social swimming, the better his long-term chances. You must help him learn what most boys seem to learn on their own: how to choose possible social partners in his peerage, think of appropriate shared activities, encourage social interest, learn from his attempts, take social risks, and make appropriate social gestures.

Once the person shows interest in more outgoing social activities, a practical way to help either gender is to encourage them to initially think of dating as another activity to be done with social associates. The "date" can simply be an activity with a friend of either sex, without an adult directly present. They can share watching a movie, a game or other mutually enjoyable activity. The pragmatic side of this social experience sharing is to decrease fear of rejection and perhaps, more willingness to try at all.

The next chapter deals with surviving the first period of sexual awakening in adolescence. For both genders, survival until a saner adult period arrives may be as good as it will get.

Surviving the First Wave of Sexual Interest

Most of our people will be lucky to survive the first wave of sexual interest among their peers. They can survive and eventually join this group's "social migration," but they will rarely join it as early or with as much confidence as their classmates. In the long run, the best that most of them can hope for is an initial feeling of isolation that eventually improves as they learn what is far less confusing to their peers.

For a young man or woman, there is a time when one hears more talk among peers, about things like people beginning dating, and what that "may" imply. This is an initially exciting period for all. It is shared around the locker room, school bus, before school, after school, in or out of class, and any time that students can talk freely.

Sex is like a wave. Within every young community, it starts with one pebble dropping into a social pond. More pebbles join and an inevitable wave of group social exploration rushes over everyone. Those who ride the wave rule. Those who can't keep up feel as if they drown in the relative power of the wave and don't understand the current.

That first wave of social and for some, sexual activity, involves most of our peers but leaves those on the spectrum behind. The relative naiveté of autistic girls or their possible wish to trade sex for "popularity" may initiate them far earlier but rarely in a healthy way. Just because one allows herself to be used as a sexual appliance does not mean any social development or more of a relationship than exists between a cheeseburger and its consumer.

The worst part of that first wave is how it destroys any feeling of acceptance, hard-won from years of struggle and the support of the best intervention and education available. One learns within a year or so that despite any classroom progress, that in the eyes of peers, he or she is socially undesirable. The result is but one more reason to be an outcast and target of humiliation.

That is how many of our people will experience puberty in school; left behind and alone and feeling steadily worse about it. People who had time for you before, now don't. That time is now shared with people who go around in groups of social pairs. There are rumors of social and even sexual activity that usually only serve to make our kids feel more left out. True, the people telling the stories are usually not nearly as active as they claim to be. Listening to a group of schoolboys in the locker room is like listening to a blind man teach defensive driving. But to the people totally left out, especially autistic boys who have little personal experience to compare with what they are hearing, it sounds true enough. Media doesn't help. TV and movies rarely show enough attention to anything but the main event. The little steps that lead to sex just aren't seen as very interesting.

The bottom line is this: in high school and even middle school, the first sexual wave transforms the student body. They measure themselves and other peers by the perceived amount of social and sexual attractiveness. This often translates into a pecking order of who gets teased and ridiculed. Many adults with autism suffer from post-traumatic stress induced from the pain of this period. This must not be allowed to happen!

So far, puberty has been described by your male author. It is also experienced by females on the spectrum, although in different ways. It is time for the wise comments of my co-author and wife.

It doesn't take a rocket scientist to tell you that puberty can be hell. Not only for an autie or aspie, but for just about everyone. Suddenly, our hormones are totally redefining and reshaping our entire universe.

Sensations and emotions overwhelmingly surge through our bodies and minds. The shapes of our bodies and social worlds suddenly change. We're expected to be adults and children at the same time. Adults demand one strict code of behavior and appearance while teen peers demand another. At the same time we are pressured to do well at school.

For those of us on the spectrum, it can be an unsolvable puzzle. We have a social communication disability. We've already had a hard enough time communicating with our peers in childhood. Back then, our parents and educators went to great lengths to encourage and educate us to be like other children. The rules were simpler. If one game of checkers was lost, a fresh, new board could be set up and you could win the next game. A wide array of games could be engaged in, in lieu of actual social opportunity to observe normal social behavior and learn how to imitate it. At this point in life, some people find shelter in their studies. Many of us are not capable of that. Some of us regress. The bombardment of hormonal, social and academic changes can be so over-stimulating that areas in which we functioned well before can be diminished or lost. If that isn't challenging enough, the hormonal changes can initiate temporal lobe epilepsy or permanently diminish language, math and behavioral skills.

(Although the problems caused by temporal lobe epilepsy can be profound, it frequently goes undiagnosed because it can happen without any outwardly detectable seizure. Because onset is frequently at adolescence, it may be mistaken for teen angst and academic rebellion.)

So what do you do when this "tidal wave" of problems sweeps you away? It's just like being at the beach. If you are out in the water and just stand still or swim without paying attention, a big wave is sure to come along and smash you under tons of turbulent water. You're going to get water up your nose and you could be injured, if not drowned. You might learn to hate the ocean and never get your feet wet again. To avoid this happening, you have to watch the waves and if you see a big one, either run like a big chicken or get on top of it and ride it. If you ride the wave, it can be very exciting and fun.

Your teen years are like that. Either they can be hell and emotionally damage you forever or they can be exciting and happy. Look around at the other kids. What are they wearing? What are the hairstyles? What music do they enjoy? Copy them. But never copy any criminal behaviors. Face it. If you dress and behave differently, you might as well wear a shirt with a target printed on your back. It is very likely that you will be shot with anything from a spit-wad to a wisecrack and laughed at, bullied and even beat up.

Adults follow this rule, too. They all dress very similarly at work and play. They just tend to forget how important it is for teens to have the same rule of survival. We do not claim that "clothes make the man," but it can help to make the man or woman fit in better. Our kids have a tough enough time without sending them to school with colors that don't match and stripes clashing with plaids. Your chances of general happiness are greater if you can do something to lessen the persecution level by dressing so you fit in with your peers.

It is best if you can adopt good camouflage by your first day of school, because no matter what you do, there are some mentally *deformed bullies who will not give up their victims. Once they have spotted their prey, they will not give up their pursuit. They are very sick, insecure and sadistic individuals in need of mental health guidance. If you find that the level of mental illness and bigotry in your school is just too high to overcome, you might do well to convince your parents to transfer you to another school. You could make a better first impression and have a chance of attracting fewer predators.*

Mary's comments on dress are right on! I always prided myself on being an individual, but I must agree with her that in order to survive, you have to make some compromises on your style of dress in school. Even though teens are very rigid on dress, there are enough variations in the acceptable styles that you can find something to live with, even if you don't love it. It is worth it. If you are going to dig in and rigidly insist on doing everything your way, all of the time, you are in for a miserable time in school and in adult life, too. Everyone, no matter how talented, has to make compromises! Even a star athlete has to play the game at the agreed time, not when he would like to play it.

As both of us have pointed out, even though puberty ushers in a lot of pain, there are ways to help a person survive these painful times. But none of us can do this all ourselves. Somebody at home has to be watching and listening. An apparently happy teen, any teen, can just "give up" socially and spiral out of control, deep into depression and worse, suicide, at a frightening speed. Parents and friends need to notice when people just aren't "acting like them-selves." Once it is obvious that a person feels left out, it is time for the family to begin discussions about social and sexual curiosity. It is also important to address feelings of social inadequacy and how to cope with them.

The family must immediately address any decrease in personal happiness or self-esteem caused by the onslaught of puberty. A young, discouraged person must be reminded of his value at home and that time is on his side. He will not be locked in middle school forever or even high school! It is important to help a left-out child find other things to enjoy and maintain his self-image until he is ready to try dating.

The initial problem of social isolation is more than problems getting a date. Not all school activity is centered on dating. A per-son who is not dating can earn a place in school and still maintain their self-esteem by finding interest groups. That can be clubs, music or sports. Team sports may be not for you. Many of us are not inclined to be part of a sport where we are part of a process that is athletic but still requires social communication. Good ones to consider are track, cross-country, gymnastics and swimming. They are all intense, individual sports that combine the perform-ances of skilled individuals into team results. For the non-athletic, there are also activities like the math club, school newspaper, chess club, stage crew, photography club, band, choir, etc.

Exercise is great at any age. Even a high school autistic person is still not normal, neurologically. Exercise can help him feel more at ease, more focused, more able to handle multiple stimuli and more sure of himself, whether he wins a letter in anything or not. Besides, being healthy and looking that way is just good sense. Done as part of a group, as something the person enjoys, this can lead to making more associates and that is true for all clubs and shared high school group activities. The other benefit of this is that one's effort to be part of school life will usually be noticed and appreciated by some peers and reduce the level of ostracism leveled at a person.

You don't even have to be good at an interest to enjoy such a group. They always have some people who are really good at the activity but others who just enjoy it. Shared interests make it easier for our people to find more associates, maybe friends or even dates. Having one thing in common is a good icebreaker. My knowledge and interest in sports, mathematics and other studies helped me somewhat fit in and made me feel like my input was worthwhile. But this book isn't about me, much as I am tempted to dredge up every personal experience to "help" you!

You may not be as lucky as I was. Some of you feel as if the atmosphere at your school is not safe or tolerable anymore. If you are constantly teased, bullied and hate going to your school, you need to find a better place to finish your high school education.

That may mean going to school at home, switching to another high school or getting your Graduate Equivalency Diploma at a local junior college. This can happen for a lot of reasons but you can only tread water for so long. If you are drowning in the cruel social atmosphere of your school, something has to change.

Please exhaust all possible solutions before changing. Some schools have good bully-awareness programs, peer-buddies and other ways to make your day a lot safer and enjoyable. But some don't and need to have them implemented. You and/or your parents can appeal to have such a program installed at your school. It is important that you and your parents communicate so they can estimate when and if you are no longer safe at school. They have to talk to the school about it. It doesn't always work. Some school administrators are very receptive, but others are not. The important thing to remember is that you have a right to be safe when at school.

If a change is needed, and if you are old enough, a junior college may be the best path. Many junior colleges have programs for those who are still not high school graduates. Students are more mature and tolerant there. Bullies are rare because they aren't going to pay to attend school. The students will be older and more advanced socially, and their focus on learning makes it far less likely that you will have a problem. You should be in a safe environment there. In enough time, you will be as old as most of the students at a junior college. There are also lots of clubs and activities. You can often work part-time on campus and grow in that way. It is a good way to go if regular school is unsafe and you have exhausted all avenues to make necessary changes.

Home schooling may be for you. However, remember that you aren't being bullied because of low IQ, but because of low social awareness, which home schooling could worsen. Part of why most young autistic people have social difficulty is our rigidity. We often want to control what is done and talked about. That has to be given up if one does anything communal. Social interaction is a partnership, a sharing. Home-schooled children, particularly an only child, generally don't have to learn how to share. Those with brothers and sisters will be "blessed" or forced to share attention, toys and parent time. However, it still is not as demanding as the social challenges and opportunities of a school. Church activity and other neighborhood recreational activities can be very helpful to offset the loss of social interaction in a school. This alternative may be worth a try and the benefit could far outweigh any negative social impact. Anything beats daily torture in an irresponsibly run public school.

[Note to parents. The lure of the safety of home school may be very appealing, but there is another factor to consider. Do you have the time (count on about six hours per day) and educational background to be an effective teacher to your son or daughter? Be sure that you are not creating a person who is safe, but very far behind academically.]

Moving to another school may work temporarily, but you can't move away from your social demons if you just move from one group of social predators to another. In enough time, the signals you send about yourself may invite the new students to abuse you just as you were in your old school. It may be that you are in a special class or have a visible aide walking with you. Anything different about you will be seen as an invitation to exclude and ridicule you.

Either way, this chapter has an important lesson: You will probably feel overwhelmed and left out when most of your peers move on to social exploration and sexual experimenting. You will survive long enough to join them. That will be much easier if you find interest groups in your school and after school. Use them to keep your friends, make new ones with whom you share an interest and preserve your values.

Remember, it is your life and you have a right to enjoy it. However, it is also the responsibility of you and your parents to make it the best that it can be. No one will do it for you. Your parents will choose the best setting for your education and it is your responsibility to make it work. Retain this attitude and your chances of growing in confidence enough to be socially successful are very good. Obviously there are no guarantees, but you have the tools to enjoy your teenage years as you have a right to be spending them.

It is time to move to other important chapters. If you are a parent, reading this in an effort to help your child, later we will discuss how to decide when to begin a dialogue about sex and what to say about it.

What Should Parents Say and When Should They Say It?

As I said earlier, my parents dropped the ball on this one. I needed information on sex. I also needed to know that it could be a healthy part of my life despite my teenage insecurity. I didn't get a shred of that at all. Judging from what I have heard at many conferences, I fear that Mother and Dad have lots of company.

The details of my sex education, or the lack of it, are not important. My parents put up with me enough to earn their spot upstairs. Let's move on to your situation. If you are one of us, maybe your parents haven't talked with you yet about sex. This chapter may help you understand some things while they fuss over how to "break this news" to you! If this is the case, read this chapter and tell your parents that you are getting older and that sex is an area of interest for you. Tell them that you simply hope that it can be discussed with them openly. I think they will appreciate your concern, come through for you, and have a good conversation. Good interaction for all of you.

You may be a parent. Good! You beat your kid to this chapter. No need for a birds and bees talk with you. You obviously know that. What concerns you is what to say to a son or daughter and when to say it. By reading this, you take a good step. There are lots of great people trying to help those of us on the autism spectrum, but some stuff is just better handled in the family and this subject is one of the most important.

In many families, parents seem to hope that sex will be something they can avoid. That may be true in your family. However, there is a lot more to being a good parent than writing checks to all of the vendors. Some things you have to just do yourself and talking about sex is one of them. The first thing you should do is look for signs of curiosity in your child about sex or signs of any knowledge of it. You may see this before you get word that the school-nurse or some other public person is going to give the "sex talk." That is usually in late elementary or middle school. I was an elementary school librarian and heard this talk several times. The "sex talk", as I have heard it, is the secular, publicly funded, "Mechanics Illustrated" version; how to do it without catching AIDS. Signs are often there long before the sex talk at school. Mary knew the "facts" at an earlier age than I learned, and it still seems that girls learn this stuff faster. But Mary will handle the female side of this subject. The important thing is to notice signs of sexual curiosity, and interest.

One sure sign is masturbation. It can start at a pretty young age and, although dads may not like to think about it, it will involve girls as well as boys. An interesting point here is that this is probably one area where our young people are often as progressive as their peers. The drive begins stimulating interest. The masturbating touch feels good and, unlike normal sexual activity, does not require a partner. We can do this very well alone!

The interest in satisfying this "excitement" in our bodies by masturbating will probably begin in junior school, if not sooner.

If it is discovered, it is important not to make a child feel dirty for doing it. Explain that it is a normal, but very private, act.

There are other signs of boyhood sexual curiosity. My dad found a *Playboy* hidden under my bed. That was certainly a sign! (Sure, I only read it for the great intellectual articles and never noticed the photos!) Your child may show increased desire to see movies or TV shows in which sex plays a big role. You may notice that sites have been accessed via your computer web browser. If your child can surf the net, there are parental controls that can keep him or her out of unapproved areas.

Other signs may surface as a slogan on a T-shirt, a sticker on a schoolbook cover or simply something he says. If none of these things happen by the age of twelve, you can assume that simply by going to any school, your son or daughter has been exposed to some discussion or knowledge of sex, shared by his peerage. Most public schools are introducing the subject by the end of fifth grade and are supposed to let you know when this happens.

31

Children are supposed to have your permission to get the "sex talk." If you can hear it or see a transcript of it, this will give you a good idea of what your child knows. But you have to find out what he just thinks he knows and really doesn't. Ignorance in the name of lust is dangerous.

The time will arrive, whether you want to face it or not, when talking about sex is appropriate. The first thing is to find a comfortable time and place to talk about it. Begin by asking your son or daughter to tell you what they do know. (You may learn some things!) Reassure them that it is okay to know the "facts of life." Correct them in the places where their knowledge is not accurate, but be sure to do so in a non-condescending manner. You don't get "parent points" by making your child feel foolish.

There is an important area that schools don't address. They don't talk about ethics or responsibility because our sexual value system depends on the religious faith of each family and its cultural background. Obviously, it would not be fair to have a view based on any one faith taught to all students in a public school. Therefore, the "talk" stays pretty much to functional factors and ethics or morality is not a theme.

If your child attends a parochial school, they may get some instruction in responsibility and ethics. It is very important for you to know if and when such instruction is given and what is being shared at school. You may totally agree with what the school shares, but even if that is so, your child must also hear this from you. He needs to know that what he learned at school is important and is a serious subject.

For your daughter, it is possible to be too early, but that is better than too late. Once you begin a dialogue, it should be a life-long process of open communication. If you wait until it seems absolutely necessary, it is probably a bit too late. Children talk about sexual things way before puberty. They consider it their secret domain. After all, they often are punished if they are caught talking about it in any way. This is why they will often feel embarrassed and unreceptive when the parent finally gives the birds and bees talk.

It is certainly a challenge to judge when and what to tell an autism spectrum person and depends more on their emotional and cognitive age rather than physical age. The timetable of maturing sexually, socially and intellectually can vary a great deal. Probably the easiest, least invasive way to educate your child is with age-appropriate literature that you as the parent feel is at their level of understanding. It's pretty easy to find tasteful, scientific books of this sort.

I knew all about sperm, eggs, gestation and birth by the second grade. But I thought the sperms just floated from the father to the mother while they were asleep together. I knew never to fall asleep too close to a male, because sleeping together caused pregnancy.

It was while I was in the sixth grade that I began having my periods. Not only was having my period a shocking experience, I was also amazed to find out that I could have gotten pregnant. I can't recommend more strongly the importance of talking to your daughter about her body changes and at least the basic facts of life before she has her first period. Without warning and reassurance, this can be a frightening experience. For young men, I agree with Jerry, watch for signs of interest and curiosity. I would also recommend a talk before the school begins its series. It doesn't have to be comprehensive, just basic. A parent can go too far and make it even more complicated than it has to be.

(I am reminded of the story of the child who went to his Mother and asked, "Where did I come from?" The Mother called in Dad and they launched into great detail about the conception and birth process. The young boy looked somewhat confused, and then with a frustrated look, said, "No, no, I just want to know where I came from, like Johnny comes from Chicago, what about me?")

As we said, neither Mary or I, had the benefit of a talk at the right time. Both of us wish that our parents had used the following guidelines. It would have made the sexual world far less threatening or surprising.

Here is a list of topics to use that should be very helpful to your son or daughter. You will note that the subjects go beyond a "birds and bees" discussion. For our kids the social topics are every bit as important as the sexual. We, and professionals who have counseled on this book, feel that both parent and child will benefit from this interaction.

1   Using a picture from a physical manual, explain the functions of sexual parts, both male and female. (If you cannot find one, just following this chapter is a simple one you could use.)

2   Discuss that sex is a part of growing up and is acceptable as a topic of discussion at the proper time and place (not casually at the grocery counter!)

3   Responsibility for one's actions in seeking and having sex.

4   The importance of respecting the wishes of possible sexual partners.

5   Discuss how sexual drives have to be moderated by responsibility.

6   Hygiene, birth control and disease prevention.

7   Talk about the feeling of being left out because of lack of social participation. Great time to talk about other ways to

have social activities. (See #10.) For young girls, stress the importance of not ever using sex as a new means of gaining popularity. When you are teenager wanting very much to be accepted, this can be a problem. (We reinforce this in another chapter.)

8 This is also a good time to reinforce the fact that you are there for them to discuss anything that comes up of a social or sexual nature. It is important that they feel the connection to family support when they feel left out or confused.

9 Reassure your son, or daughter, that they will hear many "locker room tales" about the relative importance of genital mass, baseless bragging, and other sexual myths. We have found that half of what our peers told us was not true at all and the other half exaggerated. Good time to use the term, "Be skeptical."

10 Discuss the things that he or she likes to do and ways to incorporate that into social outings, either within the family or with friends. You may discuss your own first dates, early teenage social life and, if appropriate, any mistakes you may have made. Talk about you found mutual interest groups and relate it to their life. You and they can discuss places where acquaintances and possibly future friends may be found.

The bottom line is that this subject is not a one-shot deal any more than good sex is a one-night stand. It is a very important responsibility: You should introduce the subject as your way of respecting that your child is getting old enough to know about it and will have the benefit of your experience, understanding, and support.

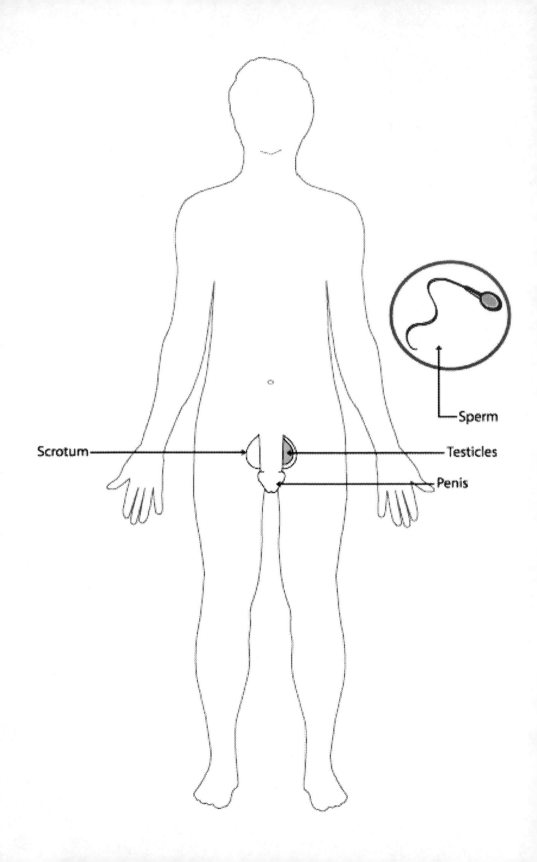

Sperm

Scrotum

Testicles

Penis

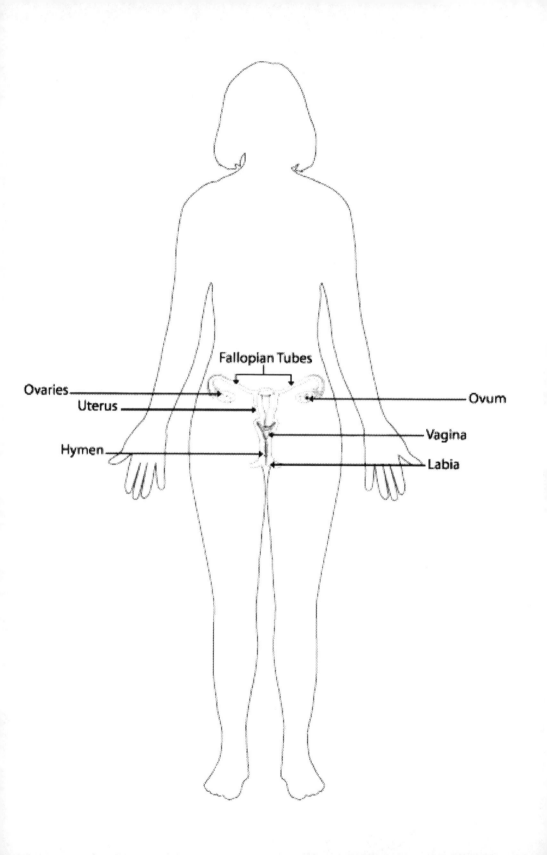

Fallopian Tubes

Ovaries

Uterus

Ovum

Vagina

Hymen

Labia

The Best Way to Date Someone is to Be Yourself

The hardest thing for many of you is to understand that the natural you is the "you" that has the best chance socially. You will probably start trying to date after most of your peers have already started. Their relative experience will be intimidating. You may have also had "friends" (not!) that have said negative things about you. It is important to put this false information aside. The experiences they told you are probably exaggerated, and their criticisms are not valid. The truth is this: you are you. What you should pay attention to are grooming and social graces and ways to present the most attractive "you" possible. However, you can't pretend to be someone you aren't. You can't live a lie, and a lie like that is so transparent that everyone will see through it.

Folks on the spectrum can be really dense about this. "Bob" is an example. Bob is an excellent runner, good enough to be considered for college cross-country and track scholarships. Bob is also tall, good looking and intelligent. But Bob isn't satisfied with that attractive reality. Bob is obsessed with totally impressing any woman he seeks with tales of his track prowess.

Now, I happen to know something about track myself - experience gained when I weighed a lot less. Bob, to put it mildly, stretches the truth about his running performances. Not only that, but track is all he wants to talk about to any new person. Result? No results! He totally fails and can't understand why. Most people won't catch him tripping up on his track claims as I do, but all of them sense the unattractive desperation of someone who talks incessantly about himself in an effort to make a big impression.

It is natural to be nervous about dating the first time, or even the second. Even experienced daters still feel nervous when they meet someone new and sense that the potential is there for a relationship. That is natural. The way to deal with this is to relax about the situation. Minimize your expectation. You will have fun. If your date has fun too, great. Maybe he or she will go out with you again. If not, at least you had fun and have lost nothing by going out.

The first thing to think about is this: What would you like to do if you had a chance to go out on a date or spend any informal time with someone? That is the first question to answer. If you like to go to games and movies, fine. If you don't, then don't do what I did. Don't do what you don't enjoy just because everyone else seems to enjoy it. You are you. They are them. Pick as many activities that you like as you can. Make this your short list of possible things to do with another person.

This sense of what you like to do is very important. If you have a good idea of what things you like to do, it makes you look more confident. A social prospect, someone you want to date, will say "yes" more frequently to someone who acts as if he knows what he wants to do. Confidence is attractive. If there are things that you enjoy doing by yourself, then do that until you find someone to share them with.

Make it easy for yourself. When you ask someone to go out, suggest an activity that you like doing enough that you would do it alone if the invitation is declined. If you are attracted to an individual who really loves to do things you hate, like sitting in a crowded, loud gym watching sports, or going shopping for doilies, then it is best to be realistic and find someone else. You have no chance with someone if you can't enjoy doing some activities together. The bottom line is: you have to know what you like to do and find people who feel the same way. You can't make yourself over to please somebody, no matter how much you would like to in order to please them. If you do, you will eventually end up disliking them because of a decision you made to abandon your own interests.

Take a good look at yourself. There must be some activities that you share with other people. As we said earlier, look for clubs or places where people share those activities. If you like chess, join a chess club. You may not meet a person to date there, but you will probably make some friends. One of those new friends might introduce you to someone to date. That is often how social connections happen.

The first date is critical. You should always pick an activity in which you and the other person both feel comfortable. You may wind up doing most of the talking but don't do all of the talking. Show some curiosity about this new person. That makes it a lot easier for her to put up with occasional horn blowing from you. In general, bragging and boasting impresses nobody. It is good to take pride in what you do well, but don't spend a ton of time advertising it.

If you are the one paying, remember that your wallet needs comfort, too. The "big first date" is a bad idea. Don't waste your money on an all-out effort to impress somebody who is new. Save the wine and roses for when it's worth the effort!! Unless you are a well-known millionaire, most women will wonder why you are spending so much money on a new date and what you expect in return. That will make them feel uncomfortable. Start simple with social activities that you can afford to continue if this first date leads to more dates. If you are the one being taken out, be considerate of the finances of your host.

By knowing what you like to do and seeking similar people, you eventually meet someone to date or a friend who may know someone else like you and helps the two of you meet. Common interest groups have great potential for friends. We understand that some of you readers may feel too shy to even go to a meeting of an interest group. I know what it is like to feel that shy, but you have to accept that real living involves some risk taking.

I am not a big fan of dice. I can find a better return on my wager in other gambling ventures. But I have learned one thing from rolling dice and watching other people do this: You have absolutely no chance of winning unless you roll the darn things! In other words, no matter what you try to do, you can't win unless you take a chance. The alternative is to take no risk. Sadly, this "don't try" attitude is alluring to some of our crowd. The result of doing nothing is predictable. You stay right where you are. But you never get where you might like to go either.

Maybe you don't see your sexual interest as a win or lose situation, but many people do. Regardless of how you view an outcome of seeking sex, you have to take a risk. You can't sit around agonizing forever on what to do. Just do something. Almost anything is better than doing nothing at all. I am not saying this as someone who enjoys looking or feeling like a fool. That has happened to me many times and still does. But I never would have found a mate or a good job or anything else worthwhile in life without taking a risk.

Trying is what's most important. Even people who are known for their enormous success universally share failure. Many times, Michael Jordan made the winning shot of a game, but he also missed many times. Mark McGuire struck out more times than he hit home runs. Even President Reagan sought that office twice and lost, before he won in 1980. Failure, once it's properly accepted and recovered from, creates character and determination. You get nowhere, vocationally, academically, socially or sexually, if you don't try. Trying is scary because when you try and fail, as all of us do at times, you give up that illusion that you could have made it if you decided to give it a try. You can always say, "I could have, but...." Once you try, that excuse is gone and the real results are the final judge.

Fear of failure is still part of my personality, but not destructively so. I have learned to voluntarily change jobs, living spaces and other parts of my life. It involved a risk in each case and some discomfort, but it was worth it even when the results were less than desirable. In risking, you gain a confidence that only comes from leaving the secure beach and riding the waves of chance. Even in failure, you know that you had the guts to try, and must give yourself credit for that!!

Take heart though, for in the social swim, fear is universal to all new swimmers. Everyone must endure the first time that you ask someone else to share your company, a date. Nobody wants to feel rejected, but it is important to learn that rejection is often really not that at all. Many times, you will ask someone out and if that person wasn't already busy or had a boyfriend, she might have said "yes." You should not take every "no" as a rejection and a disapproval of you as a person. That is easier for me to say but it is true.

There are advantages to hearing such words as "No," "Sorry, but I am busy," and similar answers. For one thing, you don't have to waste time on that person if you hear it three times. That has been my personal "Three Strike" rule. First strike, that's okay. It doesn't hurt to try again unless the other person has responded with something like, "If you were the only human on the planet, I would date another species."

After the second strike, you should stop and think. The other person obviously knows you are interested in going out. So assuming the other person has any interest in you, you will at least hear something like, "Call me next week, and we can think about getting together," or something similar to encourage you. If you haven't heard at least that on the second try, then I would give up.

Three strikes? Forget it and move on. One good way to handle this poor judgment on the part of the person you were willing to spend time with is to say to yourself, "Well, that was their loss!"

Another way to make this easier is to have another plan if you don't get a date. You were planning to use that time for fun, right? So, go ahead and have fun! You can go to a movie alone or with friends who don't have dates either. Just because some girl or guy didn't have the smarts to accept your offer shouldn't ruin your evening.

You will feel better and there is no telling what may happen if you loosen up and venture out into the social world on your own. Lots of people meet new friends that way. They meet at poetry readings, in the lobbies of theaters and art galleries, at restaurants and all kinds of other social places. And, while you are enjoying yourself, that is when you just may get lucky. That is when we all look our best and most attractive to other people.

Don't limit your enjoyment to activities with dates. Don't define whom you are and what you like to do by what the other sex will do with you. Your independent spirit as someone who can do things on your own will make you more attractive.

In fact, you can use the activities you do alone to plan how you would be on a date. For example, the next time you go to a movie theater, ask yourself: If I were on a date, where would I want to sit? In the back, the middle or the front? To the side or in the middle of a row? Where are the bathrooms, both male and female? Where are the refreshments? Where is the emergency exit?

These are structured, physical things about places where you may take a date. Having this advance knowledge will make you feel more confident when you don't have to think about these things at the last minute. Before you ever go on a date, you will get exposed to many places, movies, ballparks, and museums, etc. where older people are going on their dates. Get to know those places so you will feel comfortable with them.

For example, it is good to consider safety. Start with the way you would get to a place for a date. If it means taking a bus, then you make sure that you sit in a part of the bus that is not near where lowlife jerks are sitting. If you get on the bus and see a bunch of young strangers in the back, avoid them and sit near the driver.

If you are driving, you should know where to park. If it is a big parking lot, make a note of which aisle and space you parked in. That will save you from looking like a fool later as you look for your car while your date gets upset at you! If parking means a long walk to the movie, front gate or door of the restaurant, offer your date the option of being let out in front of the place while you park. It is best to avoid exposing you and your date to the danger of walking from your car down dimly lit alleys or other routes that are unsafe. Remember, the way you handle stuff like this is not only considerate but it makes a good impression. It shows that you care about the safety of your companion.

I say that because it is very typical for most people to be nervous as they begin dating. It is especially true for our people. The more that you know about where you are going and what the place will be like, the less you have to worry about that. This will help you relax and enjoy the occasion. The less relaxed you are, the less of a chance you have to be the person who has the best chance of enjoying a date yourself.

One thing about dating is that if you don't try to do it fairly often, it takes a lot longer to learn. Imagine how much you learn any academic subject if you only went to a class once a year. Not much. The same is true in dating. All of us experience disappointments, but it is better to move on to the next attempt.

The alternative is what many of my peers do. They summon up the courage for one attempt and maybe even get lucky and get a date. But if it doesn't work out as they hoped, they sulk and don't try again, sometimes for years.

I know one very intelligent, Asperger's male who has followed that pattern for over a decade. "Mack" is far more attractive than he will ever recognize, but his self-defeating outlook and long times between dates have resulted in almost no social growth at all. He is now just older and more bitter than when I met him.

Mack and I used to jog together. He did not get much of a chance to play sports as a youth, but he is quite strong and a much faster runner than I am. We used to run with a neighbor of mine, a pretty single woman. Mack wanted to ask her out. I tried to help. I even got her phone number for him, but rather than ever take the risk, he drove me crazy, fussing and fretting about it for miles whenever we ran together.

It would have taken him far less time to just pick up the phone and succeed or fail. It is far more practical to try than to waste time worrying about what might happen. Just do it. You may get lucky.

You may not. You have nothing to lose, but if you plan to wait a year between every social attempt, you are not giving yourself much of a chance for success.

Mack is no exception. In my old community, Mack is so well known for his constant negativity that he is almost an autistic anti-cultural hero. It is funny and sad at the same time. He has way too much company in our community. His problem is not looks, lack of money, brains or anything else. His problem is that he is convinced that as he is, nobody wants him. If that is how you see yourself, you need to change it. Mack is his own worst enemy, but all I can hope is that you don't follow him down the same path. However, whether Mack ever understands or not, his many genuine qualities have won him a group of friends, no matter how hard he is on himself.

What has been said about men can be equally applied to women. It is a fact of life that you may find a date or even partner who may disappoint you. However, that is not a reason to give up without trying again. Risk is necessary. As we said for the men goes for you too: to yourself be true. Always tell the truth in your opinions and attitudes. When you find someone who likes the real you is when you have the best chance for a relationship.

If you want to find a lover, then love yourself. Find out what you want to do. Find ways to share those interests with others. Don't try to be someone you are not. Learn from the times when your dating efforts fail. Keep looking in the right places for people who inspire a genuine interest from you. Do that long enough and you will find someone trying just as hard to meet someone like you.

Male and Female Advantages and Challenges in the Sexual Arena

By this time, the reader should agree with the authors on this: people on the autism spectrum develop sexual awareness. While certainly different from their "normal" peers, individuals on the spectrum have feelings that need to be understood. Furthermore, many of us, once aware of the exciting new presence of sex among our peers, develop a desire to seek and experience social experience and sexual interaction.

This chapter looks at the person with autism or Asperger's as if she or he is a "product" and how they stack up in the "marketplace." The goal is to identify strategies to position our people so that as many potential "consumers" notice it as possible.

I will start with our male friends.

Not all males with ASD are the same, but there are some strong, general trends. Let's first discuss the positive features. With ASD, what you see is usually what you get. What you hear, whether you wanted to hear it or not, is what he meant. This honesty, although it may surprise you at times, is refreshing. They usually lack guile, the "ability" to make believe they feel a certain way or will say things just for a social impact.

This is truly a wonderful feature in all of us. Sure, some of our people can learn to bend the truth, too. It just isn't a natural thing for us. We autistic folk are honest to a "fault." However, is it really a "fault?" Maybe the "fault" lies more with a society that encourages social lying, pretending that things aren't so when they obviously are, as opposed to our people who merely speak the truth.

We are also dependable and tend to be very precise about timeliness. I rarely hear of male peers losing jobs because of excessive absenteeism or lack of a good effort. This is definitely a strong point. Being honest and dependable is a good place for any relationship to begin. They are features most women really appreciate!

Another asset that could be attractive to the right person is that we can get very focused about things that interest us, hobbies for example. This passion for a subject of mutual interest is a great way to start any friendship or relationship.

(A woman is certainly also able to make the first move. She can either hint at her interest to a man she finds attractive or politely ask him to go out, following the same guidelines we offered in the last paragraph for the men.)

Being a woman with autism or Asperger's can mean a lot of things. We can be shy and quiet, hyperactive or passive, beautiful or plain, lower IQ and genius. We can appeal to a wide variety of tastes. One thing is for sure: We not only face the same issues neurotypical women of all character types face; we also face all of the challenges of our autism. This makes it harder for us to tackle these already difficult barriers.

Some men in our support group say that autistic women have the advantage in sexual attraction and development. The evidence they cite is the presence of autistic mothers. Yet, they are usually single mothers. The same men sometimes voicing this unscientific observation have occasionally reported that they endured some sort of sexual abuse. Well, that pretty much puts autistic men and women in the same boat. It is my opinion that the advantage/disadvantage issue is a moot point.

As with anyone else in the world, even beautiful, smart people, we all depend on chance to meet the perfect mate. All we can do is try to increase the number of chances, be alert to possible prospects and try to use our social skills and our positives of commitment, honesty and loyalty to enter into good relationships.

Getting back to the men, another good point about our men is that they actually want to share decisions with social partners. They aren't as ego-driven as most men, who often insist on calling all of the shots. Many women, those on the spectrum and off, like the fact that they are given the respect to offer their opinion.

But in the beginning, it is still usually the male who will initiate the social initiation. That requires showing some self-confidence and an ability to make some simple initial social decisions.

One way to help our young men is to help them learn a few stock social scenarios. Support groups should have practice sessions in introductions. Family members can go on "dates" with their daughter or son with autism. The practice of any social activity is a good training ground.

For example, young men or women who are planning on taking a date to a movie can learn the physical dimensions of their favorite movie theater. They can do the same with stadiums, parks or other places where they may go for a social outing. A high premium must be placed on identifying possible activities that are comfortable for the male and helping him learn the outline so he doesn't have to fuss about things at the last minute. He won't forget, for example, to get napkins when he buys popcorn at the theater because that will be part of the "movie date" drill. I call this "the art of rehearsed spontaneity." It even applies to the initial phone call for a date. It works and helps him relax.

Some drills can help here. A man can remember to always thank the woman for her time and ask for a phone number, email address, or some other way to contact her. Once that is done, he needs to prepare himself for the next contact. Ahead of time, he needs to pick an activ-

*ity, a time, and a place and make a confident contact as opposed to,
"Hi, I didn't have anything else to do so I called you. What shall we
talk about? You don't want to go to a movie, do you?"*

A good hint for parents or friends who are doing social coaching is to avoid fussing over minor mistakes. Remember that this is
a time for encouragement, not for placing seeds of doubt. If there
is anything to be corrected, please state it in a positive manner.
"Yes, that is good, but it may be a little better if you added..." (The
fact is that some parents of "auties" are often overly perfectionistic
themselves.) An overbearing, critical attitude can be really damag-
ing when the goal is to instill confidence, not more self-consciousness. Parents should lighten up and expect some mistakes to happen. Like us all, they have made some "beauts" themselves.

We can often be counted on to see things in a way that nobody
else sees them. Our unusual viewpoint can be amusing and intrigu-
ing. It loses those qualities when our perspectives are constantly
offered without consideration for anyone else. Often we show a
unique sense of humor that may get a couple of good laughs. The
problem is that often we don't understand that while a little humor
lightens the mood, endless attempts at the same joke will tire out
most ears. People whose social conversation is dominated by
humor are usually seen as too immature or lacking in confidence to
be taken seriously.

Finally, guys you have the asset of being willing to commit to a relationship and stick to it. Commitment is a treasured word to many women. You could never find a group better able to make a commitment and stick to it than those on the spectrum. Change is not our favorite thing, and if we say we will adopt a role in someone's life, we will stick to it.

So far though, there are lots of virtues in our people, if properly directed and controlled in early stages. Reliability, honesty, sincerity, loyalty and potential to make a commitment are all good things that, given patience and guidance, can eventually be appreciated.

What are the downsides? First, we are indecisive and awkward at initiating a contact to ask for a date or any other social engagement. That is a symptom of lack of confidence and we discussed a few ways to overcome that.

The biggest may be the message of desperation. The line of "I've always had rotten luck with members of the opposite sex, so please be nice or I will be crushed." This very ineffective attitude may be accompanied by hyperventilated, loud, pedantic speech and general nervousness. That is NOT the way to begin a conversation. Personally, when meeting someone new, I have been known, through pulling on my hair and other nervous behavior, to go from well groomed to disheveled in less than twenty minutes.

One bit of bad news is that some of us do not know or are not able to put our passion in perspective. Intensity, too much of it, is disastrous in initial social contact. In males, especially, their focus on one subject can have a new woman, who is merely paying polite attention, looking around for the nearest exit. This can happen at adult support group gatherings. If a pretty woman shows up, she better have a strong constitution because her entry could cause an unwanted barrage of attention.

Intensity is only a practical virtue if it can be restrained initially. The female needs time to develop comfort with a new man. Eventually, she can begin to really like him and be intense about that, too, but not on the first meeting. With many autistic men, their concept of a conversation with a new woman, is more like this:

Man:	Hi. I'm Jerry.
Woman:	I'm Sally.
Man:	Sally, do you like ice cream?
Woman:	Yes, Jerry, do you?
Man:	I sure do. We have a lot in common. Can we have sex now?

Okay, that is probably overstating it! In truth, the most unsettling part of our initial interest is what usually comes with it-a nervous voice and other self-conscious behavior that shows that we are really going to be disappointed if the woman doesn't show an interest. Most autistic males are slow to approach any woman and when they finally do, it seems to come across with the desperation of the last dance of eternity at the Last Chance Saloon. An intense male can get so wrapped up in his fervent attempt to impress a woman with his knowledge (of whatever), that, while sipping on his drink, he doesn't even notice the obviously thirsty young woman.

Intensity may not be as obvious until we successfully find someone and date a few times. We can suddenly drop interest in everything else and fixate on this new person. You may say that this is the case with normal people. To a degree, I think you are right, but our people can push the natural infatuation to a much higher and impractical level. Autistic people tend to be, as Dr. Bernard Rimland describes, "high-fidelity" thinkers, mono-centric, one activity or interest at a time. When a new interest, especially a social one, enters one of our lives, we can find it very hard to remember that there were other interests before this new one.

The good side of this can translate into commitment and loyalty, but the intense interest felt is so unnatural, in comparison to how the other person feels, that they often leave because it is just too much, too soon. We are sincerely interested in forming relationships, but have to be careful to show patience and a sense of balance in our lives, particularly at the beginning.

Some of us simply can't shed the initial appearance of being ill at ease. In that case, it is best to find friends who aren't put off by this beginning discomfort, and are patient enough to look beyond that. Unfortunately, there are just so many Mother Teresa's to go around, so you're better off learning social skills and improving your self-image so you can feel better about yourself.

Another ironic occurrence is that an autistic man who seems tactilely offensive (wanting too much contact too soon) turns tactilely defensive when the partner touches him. That is very shocking in awkward moments. This is present in both genders. Men need to be aware of how this may be interpreted as rejection. It isn't, of course, but they can learn to expect certain movements to happen in a sexual encounter and not freak out, or even enjoy them, when they do.

Another downside may be a lack of grooming and occasional gross-outs such as nose picking or stooping down to the floor to retrieve and eat a fallen food item.

Mary pays a lot of constructive attention to this in her chapter on "What Do Women Want?" so I will leave it at that. Sadly, the grooming habits of some of my friends with autism would qualify them for a farm subsidy. Do not grow a crop on yourself. It is not helpful in finding dates!

Another downside is lack of awareness of social boundaries. Many of us want to talk about serious stuff right away. Some members of the opposite sex like that and some don't. We have to learn body or verbal signals that will tell us how to tell who does and doesn't want to discuss serious subjects. Some of us don't seem to understand that some subjects just don't get discussed right away, especially in public.

Social boundaries can really crumble when your date or new friend decides that they have had enough of a subject or activity. This is a huge area where most autistic men don't get it. Sometimes your date or friend just wants to get some space. At first, we tend to not give the room that is needed and then when we do "wake up" we want to immediately fix things. Often not giving the woman space so she can cool off. This is a real psychological violation. Mary and other partners tell me that this makes them feel as if their own partner is stalking them at home. It can be a big reason for breaking up a relationship when one's lack of respect for psychological space removes the partner's feeling of security.

Tony Attwood is quoted as saying that many autistic men who have partners find ones who are nurturing and willing to pick up after them. But I have rarely seen a woman do that without expecting more of something, sympathy or emotional support, in return for the love and support she pours into her autistic male "project."

In among the positives, I mentioned honesty. Well, this is a knife that can cut both ways. If a young lady really didn't take enough time to prepare herself for a date, it would be unwise to ask an autistic man how she looks, unless she is ready to hear a cheery, "You look bad, but it's okay!" I don't think they intend to be unsympathetic or rude. They really just don't understand why their honesty is sometimes not appreciated when a social answer, not the factual answer, is desired.

Many times our directness and lack of understanding of the other's position is perceived as a lack of empathy. This can be a very big turn-off in any relationship. We have to work harder at seeing the world from the viewpoint of our date, or partner. Many times, this concern can be solved by simply asking, "What is the problem, and how can I help to resolve it?" It works wonders!

Then there is the "Oh, I have autism, I am not responsible" syndrome. I know too many men who are in relationships or can't get one of any kind, who claim autism as the reason they can't improve their situation. The standard rationale is, "I can't make any change because of my diagnosis. That is the way I am." That rationale doesn't work and it isn't accurate either. All people, diagnosed or not, are able to make reasonable compromises between their absolute worldview and those of someone they love. The rationale of inflexibility comes more from a fear of change.

For a while, I was inflexible about tactile issues with Mary. I was just afraid to deal with the issue. It is one thing to know you have some fears, but if you are in a relationship, then you need to address those fears when doing nothing and staying in your rut causes great distress to your partner. From what I have heard, rigidity in that sense is a big problem for my male peers.

Sometimes, as we discussed, there are adults on the spectrum who have a problem with self-image and actually not liking who they are. When that is the case, it is hard for others to like them, at least enough to spend time socially. I have found this to be particularly true for men on the spectrum.

This is the challenge of self-esteem. It starts in the sandbox and goes up through school and into adulthood. Parents and caregivers can do a lot to build confidence and self-assurance in our people. One of the parents I know goes out of his way everyday to find something positive to say to his son. Sometimes, he has to reach for a compliment, but always finds something positive to say. It will not surprise you that this young man, although still dealing with autistic tendencies, has a very positive self-image.

However, in the final analysis, the responsibility for how we feel about ourselves is up to us. We have to understand our worth and give ourselves credit for the good things we bring to the world and those who love us. It is all too easy to labor on our negatives and not recognize how terrific we are.

I can't wave a wand over a person's life and turn it into the kind of life that results in a person with much higher self-esteem. All I can say is that self-esteem depends on a lot of positive rearing and support throughout life. We all have a long way to go in finding the optimal way to provide that for autistic people, male or female.

To sum up our view of the social "marketplace" for us auties and aspies, we have many virtues. The challenge of selling the virtues of "our package" are the barriers of self-consciousness, impatience and all the other things we need to better control in the beginnings of a social relationship. If our people can chill out enough to make a sturdy, sincere initial impression, there is enough attraction in us that in time, we will find a friend or lover (hopefully both,) who wants to take his or her "product" off the shelf and take home to Mother and Dad.

Sensory Issues in Sex!

Sex is not done, correctly, with a stopwatch in a free hand. Neither is life itself. Sometimes we on the spectrum approach everything with a somewhat frantic, get it over with, and move on attitude. We need to slow down and enjoy our experiences. This is often true with the sex act. A common complaint among many people, especially women, is that too little time is devoted to the entire sexual interaction, including what happens before, during and after.

Ideally, all senses should be involved, touching, tasting, smelling, feeling and saying loving things. Too often, they are not. I am still learning about this myself so I don't mean to preach from a pedestal of expertise. I think that in a way, the fast way in which I read, notice visual things in general and think, has hampered me in sex.

The key is to slow down and enjoy, sensually, the entire world around you. Many of us eat too fast. We don't really enjoy the taste of what we eat. The same is true even when we visit a place like a museum. I used to frustrate Mary with the way I would look at paintings momentarily and immediately go on to the next one. It is a lot more fun to really look at each painting. What is this about? What kind of mood was the artist in? What kinds of pigment were used? Does the painting or other artwork give any clue about its age? There is a lot to be observed if you just give it a chance.

Why hurry something that is fun? If you go to a concert, would you stand up and tell the band to "Get this song over with. I already know all of the lyrics!!" No. I hope you wouldn't. Most of the fans of the Grateful Dead could have said that, instead they danced all night with a band that knew no limits to length of performance or enjoyment. That is the way good sex can be; a dance you can do all night!!

Many people are so hung-up on performance that they forget that this is not the end, only a part of the whole process of mutual enjoyment. A good partner is not keeping a scorecard on whether you do everything "right" or "on schedule." Slower is better.

My pets have helped me. My dog, parrot and cat can accept as many strokes as I have time to give them. It seems that to them, petting strokes are like snowflakes; no two are alike. The same is true for loving strokes of your partner. I don't think you can over-do this. Caring for and about another person is a gift to you both.

Along with the basic sex drive comes the need to feel a warm, sensually responsive body during the act. Even though masturbation can be executed more efficiently, and release tension and bring some satisfaction, most of us are born with the additional need for the sensation offered by the presence of another person.

Some of us have a sensory challenge of being very tactile defensive, to one extent or another. Hence, since some are sensitive to touch, there is the misconception that "those on the spectrum don't want sex." For many of us, that is simply not true. However, wanting something and having any idea as to how to get it are two entirely different matters. For some, the tactile problem itself can be approached, as Temple Grandin has demonstrated, with her "hug machine" by having pressure therapy where we gradually increase touch on our bodies with a machine or someone who is a good friend or partner. Temple is a good resource on the tactile defensiveness issue and covers that issue well in her video on sensory issues (Future Horizons 1999). Some people, like my partner, have reported a reduction of tactile defensiveness from exercise, or certain medications, or meditation.

Nature outside is another facilitator for adding overall sensuality to your sexual experiences. Take the time to really enjoy a sunrise or sunset. If you jog, sit down in the morning grass and feel the moisture. Slowly stretch and slowly build up to your comfortable running or walking pace. Notice where you walk or run, the life around you, trees, hedges, birds, animals, flowers. Take a break and really smell a new flower. Give yourself enough time to remember the smell.

The more you learn to fully enjoy different activities, rather than compulsively do them, the more sensual you will be when you want to be. It will open your mind to new experiences. You may have never thought of yourself as an artist. However, you don't have to be one to have fun with it. Just take a pencil and a napkin and draw a picture of whatever you would like to see, touch, hear or feel. Draw a cartoon of how you feel at the moment. Try singing as often as you can. Even if you don't have the greatest voice, whenever it is appropriate, sing your favorite songs. The important point is not the artistic quality. The point is to liberate your senses so you can enjoy learn to express all of them.

The more you can enjoy the world around you, with all your senses of touch, smell, sight, hearing, and feeling, the more you will be able to enjoy it with someone else.

When Desire Leads to a Bad Relationship

This chapter is about bad relationships. My population is probably more likely to fall into this trap than other people because of our low self-esteem. A bad relationship is often one in which one person has their needs subverted to the ego and needs of the other person. It often results because the exploited person deludes himself or herself into thinking they have a real relationship when in fact they are being used.

My peers and I are natural suckers. For many of us, it is so hard to make a first friend that we are vulnerable. Apparently, there is something about our natural vulnerability that brings out the predator in theoretically decent human beings. I have learned the hard way that you must have limits on what you will do in the name of "friendship." If you don't, people you think are your friends will take everything you have and happily drive over you in the car they bought with the money they "borrowed" from you.

If a person isn't having any sexual luck anyway, the lure of a possible relationship is deadly, especially if it is with a very attractive, charismatic member of the opposite sex. Attractiveness is not hard to define, but as far as charisma goes, I haven't a clue. Most people and I would look at Charles Manson, the cult leader, and see a disheveled bum, but to the idiots in his flock, he was the greatest. Beats me.

Most members of the exploiting half of bad relationships have no intention of ever delivering on the wishes of their ardent friends/fans. In fact, in most instances, they make that clear from the beginning, but our people often keep on pushing into an "association" that they mistakenly think is a relationship.

Many of us don't know when to take "no" for an answer. We fixate on a person and decide that by hook or crook, we will have a special relationship with that person. Usually, our intense desire is noticed by the target, who politely informs us that our dream is unrealistic. But that doesn't stop us. We may even accept the offer of a friendship without sex, but we usually don't really mean it. Our secret agenda is to play the role of a friend, until we convince the other person that we are "the one" after all.

The odds are hugely against this happening. Chemistry was not my best subject in high school, and it is not hard to figure out why. Most people with social experience usually can sense in a short time that someone else is not an appropriate sexual possibility. That is what chemistry is all about. In the chemical sense, it is why some elements bond immediately and others never bond or instead, have disastrous reactions! In the human sense, it is the feeling that the presence of another person, however ardent, sincere and well intended, is just not a comfortable fit for you.

The good news is that if we are smart, people who can't be lovers but are good friends can help us grow socially. We can do things together and without the social pressure of expectations about the end of the date. However, that means that the person who is originally sexually interested must drop that desire. If you accept an invitation for a platonic, non-sexual relationship, you have to mean it, and stand by your word!

If you don't mean it, the result is bad for both of you. You will wind up doing lots of things that you wouldn't ordinarily do, in the hope of converting that person into your lover. When disappointed, you may feel exploited, forgetting that the other person never asked you to do what you are doing. You may say, "Look at everything I do for you that those other people don't. Why don't you appreciate me?" If you are lucky, the target of your desire will tire of this manipulation and end the "friendship," which never was a friendship anyway, because you weren't sincere about accepting it.

That is the better prospect. The other possibility is that you will be used by someone who has no intention of ever delivering on your dreams, but will toss you enough affection on occasion to keep your hopes up. Once in a while, your hard-up self will thrill to a hug or even a warm kiss, accompanied by some comment like, "I just may have been wrong about you!" or other totally manipulative messages. Either way, this is a bad relationship.

It is good to have friends of the opposite sex who are not your lovers. They can help you understand what is going on when you have a problem with a lover. If you have to survive a trauma, they are there for you. But you have to accept the boundaries of a platonic relationship in order to benefit from it.

Another common problem, especially for our men, happens when we misinterpret the professional courtesy of a woman as interest. That could be a secretary who politely talks to you, when you deliver something to her employer and wait for a signature. It could be a waitress who is paid to smile and laugh at everyone's jokes, no matter how bad they are.

We could think, "This person really likes me." Then we begin to show up at the secretary's office or the restaurant, without a good reason, hoping to converse more and initiate a social contact. This is rarely what the other person meant, and if this action persists, it can be viewed as stalking.

Another variant of this is when one becomes obsessed with another person and knows her schedule. He "accidentally" arranges, as one man did, to be just outside of her locker room when she finished with track practice. If you try that once and get somewhere, fine. Maybe she is interested. But if you show up, every day, and she never even stops to notice you, then three things are obvious to everyone: She is not socially interested. Your daily presence at the same time, same place, is no accident. And worse: You are not taking the hint. You are stalking this person, so what can happen next? What happened in the case of this man was that he was reported to the campus police. I don't blame the girl one bit for doing it. She did nothing to mislead this person and had every right to be concerned.

There is another kind of stalking, the voyeur kind. If one has no luck in getting sex, it may be enough to just be able to look at some pretty sexual objects and feast on that for a while. In one situation, an autistic person worked in a place where a couple of young women sat and studied on a daily basis. They probably chose the area because it was quiet and close to their next class.

So, the autistic person found such a visual feast too hard to pass up. He arranged his work schedule so that he would be able to look at them from what he viewed as a safe distance. He figured, "I'm just looking, and I'm not right in front of them, so why does it matter?" It does matter. It is one thing for someone to look at you and recognize that you are pretty. It is another thing to be stared at by a stranger, trying to do this in secret, for a long time, on a regular basis.

Often the visual stalker has no clue how obvious his actions are to people around him. Temple Grandin cites a hilarious case of a man who fixated on a woman in his community. He decided to stand in a field, across the street from a window of her residence, wearing a football helmet so nobody would recognize him! Nobody recognized the "peeping Tom," but it didn't prevent the peeping Tom in the football helmet from being busted!

Stalking is not just a male problem, but it seems that it is a lot harder to accuse or prove a female of stalking than a man. The main reason for this is that men do it so obviously, that they get caught. If a woman does it, she is usually much more discreet. It is not a wise thing to do and it indicates social desire or frustration that needs to find a more constructive expression.

Whether it is stalking or, as in the case, which started this chapter, one's refusal to accept the non-interest of another person, autistic people are prone to getting into trouble because of their social perseveration. They have to learn that if a person says no, that is what is meant. It is far better to accept the truth than to try to manipulate it into something that will never be, or in the case of stalking, literally "rape" someone by forcing your unwanted attention on them.

It actually can get worse. In extreme cases, a person may totally lose his feeling of self-worth. He may measure his value by a friendship or association with someone whose attractiveness, etc. makes him feel good to be seen or associated with her. To keep such a relationship alive, no matter how parasitic the other person is, that person will do anything. Our people are particularly vulnerable to this because of the low self-esteem many of us face.

Social addictions don't even need personal contact. Not with the Internet. Some autistic people think that an exchange with someone, prompted by an Internet discussion group, means social interest. They can get completely hooked on somebody who lives a continent away, is married, and has no interest in anything but interesting conversation.

The sad truth is that the tendency of autistic people to misread social cues makes them vulnerable to going off the deep end in pursuit of a perceived social interest that doesn't exist. Part of this is from social misunderstanding, but part of it, as we get older, is from a desperate resolve to try literally anything. In an age when many people begin dating in middle school, it is not uncommon at all for autistic people to be in their twenties and older without such an experience, let alone any sex. The longer they go feeling left out, the worse they feel about it, and the poorer their judgment becomes.

You may find a person stuck in one of these relationships, either the kind where he is being passively exploited or has developed an addiction to being around another person. It is difficult to "save" these people. The best thing you can do is to keep the communication open. Be there for him or her when, as usually happens, the reality of the "non-relationship" becomes apparent to your friend. They usually have to bottom out, lose all hope, and reach out before they find a way out of these sick situations. Other things a caregiver or friend can do are mentioned in other chapters; help to create social alternatives, teach dating and relationship skills, be there to listen and encourage, etc.

Please remember that many of you neurotypical people go through similar waves of anguish when relationships go the wrong way. Our people just go through it deeper and with more confu-sion.

What Do Men Really Want?

Editor's Note: Obviously anyone can read this, but it is primarily intended only for young women considering a relationship. We recommend adult guidance.

First, it is fair, although not complimentary, that for many young men, the drive is to collect as many romantic and sexual adventures for their scrapbook as possible. Then, ironically, men want to settle down with a woman who is so important that they would never treat her like all the women from their sexual scrapbook.

Obviously, men don't really mean to be boorish, but they have to be untrained from negative sexual images that originate from the way they first learn about sex. Young men may be full of stuff like "James Bond" movies (or the modern equivalent) or other cultural influences that say you should be a great "stud," have lots of lovers and be a "man of the world." Promiscuity in men is often seen as an attribute, but they can be totally hypocritical when it comes to women.

The same man who may be very proud of his sexual track record will often want to think of himself as the first and only man to have sex with you. This is the same man who will look to you as the one who will settle him down to a permanent, monogamous relationship, focusing all of your attention on him.

This is a male fairy tale. The only way to make it a reality is to believe that 99% of single women are virgins and the "studs" acquire their extensive sexual experience and prowess from an incredibly busy 1% of the women in your community. It is a sillier fairy tale than Peter Pan, but many men seem to believe in it (or at least pretend that they do).

As a woman, you can win temporary "popularity" by literally "spreading yourself around," having sex with a number of men. But that popularity is only for the few times that you sleep with any of these people. Once they have tired of you, they will want a woman who isn't so "easy." There is a huge difference between being popular because you are "accommodating" and being someone who is respected. I assume you don't want to try the option of being disrespected, however tempted you may be by the temporary "popularity," of giving up your virtue.

Not all men want the same type of woman, but there are strong trends among males. Men are taught to make most initial social decisions. They are supposed to be the hunters and you, the hunted. Some men will actually feel awkward if you are the one to ask them to go out. Others will be very complemented. So, when dealing with men, you have to be careful and be sure to go slow. Some guys may think that if you ask them out, this means you are easy. If they go out with you, they may have great expectations about that first evening, even sex on the first date, which is a bad idea!

This doesn't mean that you can't ask a guy out. We only offer this as a "heads up" as to how some men think. A little later, we discuss asking a guy out.

Having sex on your first date is really foolish, no matter how much you think you like the person. He will wonder, "Does she do this with every man she goes out with? What kind of disease can I risk getting? Is she so hot for sex that she will just sleep with the first man available when I am not around?" These are not the kind of messages you want a man to receive. A man may wish to collect his "experiences," but he wants to feel as if your experience with him is special and not available to just any man. Maybe that seems hypocritical, but most men think that way and always have.

But if you like someone and think that he is too shy to ask you to go out, it is all right to ask him to have a cup of coffee or do some simple activity together, with the chance of that leading to a first date. You should have a reason to do this; some contact with the person already, a conversation that may have indicated an interest in you. Don't just pick a random guy in your school hallway and ask him out. That will get you an undesirable reputation as rumors can spread fast, and unfairly, around your school or neighborhood.

Your inner self is most important, but your exterior looks can repel many good potential dates if you don't pay attention to your appearance. There is no excuse for poor hygiene and a sloppy appearance. I am informal and so is Mary, most of the time. There is a huge difference between informal and sloppy.

The clothes you wear should always be clean and fit you. That much is a no-brainer. There is plenty of range beyond that. However you are dressed, being neat and clean are the most important factors. More men are more impressed by a neatly clothed woman who wears a T-Shirt with an unconventional slogan than by a woman wearing expensive clothing that doesn't fit or looks like she threw it on at the last minute.

What you show or don't show has a psychological impact. I have walked on nude beaches and wanted to get some blankets to cover up most of the bathers. If you have an absolutely gorgeous body, that will be obvious without you walking around semi-nude whenever you can. How you dress and how much you wear are advertisements as to the type person you are.

Now, let's leave my recommendations for a little bit and hear from my better half, Mary. Her thoughts are from experience, not just observation as are mine.

Let's talk woman to woman. My tips are intended to have you think of yourself in the totality of your social being, not just the physical, although that is important, but also how you view yourself socially and sensually.

Hopefully, this book will expand your sexual horizons. We believe this is a good first step, but also recommend you read other books on this subject. My very favorite one is an enduring classic, called The Joy of Sex. It is fully and tastefully illustrated and easy to read. Then, there are Dr. Ruth's books. She is very open with her opinions, but is also funny and entertaining. I also suggest those written by Dr. Joyce Brothers.

There are thousands and thousands of romance novels available. Not only are they fun and stimulating to read; they can open up your social and sexual vocabulary and imagination. You can learn new romantic phrases to say. You can learn new romantic overtures and things to do that will attract and hopefully keep a mate.

The more you read and the more you gain experience, the more the meaning will likely change. If a bad experience occurs, sit back, take a deep, relaxing breath and identify the problem(s) that occurred. If a good experience occurs, do all you can to maintain it. Keep the meaning of sex as positive and gratifying as possible.

Most of us autie and aspie women, as is true with woman in general, do not resemble a sexy movie star. This doesn't mean we can't attract men. We most certainly can!

However, we do have to consider our physical looks. Much is said in this book about the importance of outward appearances. For women, there are many magazines on the subject. However, I will just briefly make a few recommendations. If you are a teen, Seventeen magazine is great. If you are an adult, Cosmopolitan and Redbook are two great places to start. Cosmopolitan gives great advice on what men want, how to get what you want out of men and career, how to apply make-up and lots of fashion pictures. Redbook is little more conservative and offers "middle-America" kind of recommendations.

If you can't quite master good make up techniques from a magazine, go to a department store cosmetics counter and get a make over kit. Very often the sales clerk will be very informed and can give you some tips. You don't necessarily have to buy their expensive products. Just learn the colors and application technique and buy a less expensive line, like Maybelline. It's available at the grocery store or the drug store. It works very well.

You can also do this at a beauty college. You will be given to a stylist who will soon graduate and be charging much more at the local beauty parlor. However, at the school, you will usually get good, supervised, service that will cost a fraction of a regular salon.

A nice, relaxing, skin-invigorating facial should come first. Especially go this route if you have skin blemishes. Your blackheads and pimples can be treated. If you are considering getting your nails done as part of your makeover, please heed this professional word of caution: do not go to a bargain nail salon! More often than not, they use MMA (Methyl Methacrylate). MMA can have a wide array of side affects including:

1. Moderate to severe itchiness and sensations of pressure on the nail bed.

2. Permanent damage to the nail bed and nail root, preventing normal re-growth. This can cause deformation of the nail..

3. Body rashes wherever the nails touch. They can range from typical red rashes to black spots to leprosy-like conditions.

4. System shock and/or death has been been reported in first-time MMA users.

MMA is illegal in most states, but is widely used in bargain salons simply because the State Boards of Cosmetology cannot enforce testing of this highly hazardous substance, due to staffing or financial restraints.

For your hair, you could try asking a beautician what would make you look better. Be sure to state your lifestyle and personality characteristics. Change can be a little shocking for us. Just give it a chance and see how other people react. If you only go by what you are used to, you might be the only person who actually likes it. Every style and color gets a different reaction.

I have done a great deal of experimentation on how people react to each hair, make up and dress style. I have made numerous visits to the same stores and restaurants wearing different wigs, dresses and makeup. I was treated differently with each style and color when I visited the same location. Sometimes, no one even waited on me! But the next time, I was a beautiful, well-dressed blonde and everyone said, "Hello, can I help you?" I'm not just kidding or exaggerating. It's true!

There is a possible problem with "being blonde." Men sometimes associate being blonde, (particularly bleach blonde) as dumb, spoiled and self-centered; a perfect prospect for a quick sex-fling. Another drawback: bleached blonde hair requires a fairly expensive visit to the salon every six weeks for a touch up. Also, hair quality can diminish. If you feel the disadvantages are outweighed by the universal, immediate appeal of the blonde, you can try it. If you don't like it, you can always go back to a darker color.

While men generally prefer that a woman be sexy to warrant the initial relationship, the truth is that many men have a hard time sustaining a relationship. Unless, of course the guy is on the spectrum! Then, he will probably never leave you. For most guys, sexual "fever" is only good for so long and then needs to be replaced by the strength of friendship and companionship.

Even if he is in love, feels he could maintain a lifetime relationship with a woman, enjoys her intellect and knows she's a great domestic and financial prospect, he can still be very fearful! He thinks that entering into a committed relationship could mean a loss of a great deal of time spent doing "guy stuff." There are fears that it will mean a life of housework, domestic existence, the dreaded shopping malls, pleasing the emotional needs of a woman and also, possibly, children. This scares a lot of men.

However, there is hope. First, some men actually like some, if not all, of the above. Secondly, if you see that he dreads shopping or whatever, you can gracefully exclude him from the things that he hates and you love. Also, you can have a crack at some of the things that he likes. You may find them interesting!

My next advice is to try some "guy stuff." They do a lot of fun, exciting things! Some of these you may already find enjoyable. If so, you're ahead of the game.

Here's a list of fun things I learned to do with guys:

1. **Physical horseplay:** Play wrestling can lead to other social activity. However, be careful, people have been known to get hurt playing around. If he gets too rough, tell him to back off.

2. **Off-Road driving:** You bounce and jostle along, seeing great scenery. You can share picnics and kisses in beautiful, secluded locations.

3. **Primitive survivalist excursions:** You match your wits and physical abilities against the wilderness. After nightfall, there is nothing to do but sit around the campfire and cook, talk and make out under the gorgeous, starry sky.

4. **Mechanical "challenges":** You might just hand tools and supplies to him or if you are mechanically inclined, you might be a working partner. Encourage him to tell you what he is doing. Guys love to impress just about anyone with their mechanical prowess. Another side benefit is that you can learn enough so that you will be "uncheat-able" when you take your own car in to be serviced.

5. **Pool, billiards, chess, and other sports:** He may take pride in teaching you, or having you join in the competition. Another mutual pastime is developed. He sees you as someone to spend recreational time with.

You're not just a female to please in order to have some sex.

6. **Watch TV and stadium sports together:** Even if it doesn't interest you, let him teach you about it. Once you understand it, it might become fun.

7. **Opinions of the world and life itself:** Learn what men really think without being politically correct. They usually like a little verbal sparring, but don't want to lose. However, if you do make a point that he disagrees with and he acts childish, take that as a good cue to find someone else.

Ultimately, you and your male friends will enjoy your time together if you find things you both enjoy. Many men can get sex easily enough, but sometimes don't actually enjoy spending time with women beyond the "conquest." Be a woman that a man actually enjoys spending his precious time with!

Dating is something that must be looked at realistically. Slower is better. It is not wise to put pressure on a social partner to hurry sex and commitment. The beginning should be unconditional fun that may lead somewhere and may not. It usually doesn't. You can't look at every new man as "the one" right off the bat. You can't sell yourself short and think that someone, on the basis of a superficial meeting, even a cou-

ple of dates, is absolutely it. When you do that, you become self-conscious and can blow a potentially good thing. The other person will usually sense that this means too much to you, too soon. He may cut things off for fear of hurting you, or he may just take advantage of your intense interest, grab some sexual action, and move on.

This is important: you must accept that it takes a while for people to decide if things are getting serious and maybe permanent. It is important to see how deep the interest is from the other person. Does he really talk to you and listen, or does he just go through the motions of conversing and try to only talk about what interests him? Do you really feel interested in him, or is he just the only man available at the moment? You can't make these decisions in just one or two evenings, but I can tell you this much: if you do enough dating, eventually you will be with someone with whom it is just easier to do everything. With the right person, you are comfortable and do not feel self-conscious. You feel that you can trust the person and that these feelings are mutual. That is the type of situation in which sex is eventually most appropriate.

You need to take stock of yourself before you hop into bed with anyone. What else do you have to offer, other than your body? Hopefully, you aren't another bra-less, blonde, "valley girl" in jeans and a t-shirt. The point is that if sex is the only thing you have to offer this guy, you had better reexamine the relationship and yourself. If the only thing happening in the relationship is sex, most of your lovers will get their fill and kick you out of bed as soon as they realize that the cartoon channel is your idea of intellectual stimulation.

Suppose you have taken your time and now have a sexual partner who is taking you seriously. Good. He will probably want to feel, even in the beginning, as if he is the most important male in your life, past and present. He will not want to spend time, hearing you talk about the other men who have been in your life. I know a few women who actually think that such a conversational line impresses men. It does not. The more you talk of your romantic past, especially if there was a sexual part, the more available, less unique and cheaper you look and feel.

If he asks you to talk about one of your ex-lovers to "help him understand you better," stop and think! Where is this conversation going? Is it really going to make your relationship better? Probably not! (Ladies, remember this is the male ego we are dealing with here.) The best answer you can give to that request is, "Compared to you dear, he was nothing!" Remember, discretion is the better part of valor. Answer as briefly as possible! The less said the better. The less time that either of you spend, talking about previous romantic partners, the better. You are both better off if you let the other person occupy the center stage of your life and attention span as much as possible.

Most men feel that they should be the ones to attempt kissing and touching in key areas. You can signal them that this is too much, in the wrong place, or that you approve, with your hands. You don't have to lie there like a mannequin and submit to anything a man wants to do. It is your body, and if an accident happens, basically it will be your pregnancy or disease, too. So, you can, (and should!) take control of who gets to kiss, touch and have sex with you.

Pay particular attention to whether a man listens to your needs and requests. If he persists in doing things that you aren't ready for or don't want to do, that is not a good sign. By going along with that, you encourage a permanent, negative pattern. You have to know that the man cares more about a future with you than he does about momentary ego gratification.

What I can say about many men, from what they have told me, is that they do enjoy some reciprocation on the part of a woman. For example, if a man is taking off a woman's bra, it is fun to feel a woman's hand on him, unbuckling a belt or touching a zipper. However, a man's style may not be what you prefer. He may want you to do things that you don't like to do. You should not do things that you consider unsafe or uncomfortable. If that is going to make or break a relationship, then it is not worth continuing.

You will make a man feel more comfortable and happier, (and you will be too!) if you are discreet enough to have one sexual partner at a time in your life. Explore that partnership thoroughly. It will take months and maybe years to decide if this should be a permanent relationship, but neither of you need the confusion or risk of multiple sexual relations. Don't let a new sexual partner get the idea that he can expect intimacy every time he sees you. There is a lot more to being and living together than sex, so make sure that once he has enjoyed that with you, that this is not the only activity that interests him.

Summary: Patience is best. Too much, too soon, usually leads to disaster. Respect yourself. Groom and present yourself as someone to be taken seriously. Show a genuine interest in a man and don't bore him with tales of your romantic past. Men want to feel special. If you make them feel that way and take your time, the chance of your next social, sexual partner being a meaningful one will be much better. Quality in sex is far better than quantity.

What Do Women Really Want?

Editor's Note: To the adult. This chapter is the most explicit in the book. You may want to be selective as to which portions you share with your child or student.

This chapter is written for men. The intent is not to titillate, but to educate. There are tips here that may help you in achieving a good relationship.

You! Yes, you. Maybe not all, or even most, women. But some woman, somewhere, wants someone just like you. So, let's get you ready for her!

First, let's make you the best you that can possibly be. Sure, lots of girls pass up the nerd type and go for the handsome football player. But they sure regret it when they end up with a womanizing, beer-swilling lout on the couch. Meanwhile, the nerd goes on to be a rich entrepreneur with exotic interests.

(Remember the words of Bill Gates, "Be careful how you treat a 'nerd' in school. One day, you may be working for him!")

To any handsome football player reading, I apologize. I don't mean you are more likely to become an alcoholic, any more than anyone else. I just mean that the inside of the person is the most important over the *long term, whether you have the advantage of sexual attractiveness in the teenage years or not.*

Not that the outer looks are unimportant. We'll get to that later. First, we want to re-establish what everyone would agree is the most important part of you, your values and ethics and what you can contribute to the world. Your principles, how you care for others, your mind, sense of humor, and compassion are all very important to anyone once they get to know the real you.

However, the reality is that few women will get past a totally unattractive, disheveled, exterior to get to the good that is inside. Perhaps if we work on your outward presentation, you will experience some nicer responses to your presence. And yes, we will frankly discuss what makes a woman interested in you physically, and keep her coming back for more.

First, we need to get you a date.

A woman makes immediate and permanent judgments based on your face, hair, and clothes. We auties and aspies have enough social challenges without carrying unnecessary burdens and stigmas which we certainly can do without. So let's go to work on your appearance - your statement of, "Hey, world, this is who I am!"

Let's go to the mirror. Give your mirror a smile of greeting. Think your happiest thoughts and see how your smile improves. This is your most important initial attribute. If you have trouble smiling at the present sight of your face, then perhaps the work we will do now will make you feel more like it by the time we are done.

Give your mirror another smile of greeting. Look closely. How are your teeth? Are they sparkling clean? How is a woman ever going to think of kissing your lips if your teeth are not clean? You must brush them every morning and evening at a bare minimum. Then, it is prudent to carry toothpicks for other meals when you can't brush.

Often, people get chicken, hamburger and other foods stuck between their teeth. Even I do. Always look for a restroom after a meal so you can check your teeth and make sure there is no ketchup or other food on your mouth, face, and clothes. Even neurotypicals must do this.

Now, if you have a beard, is it neat and the rest of your face clean-shaven? This includes under your chin and your neck. You should shave every day and take the time to examine your work closely. If you have stubble on all or parts of your face, women think two things: If you ever kiss them, the stubble will hurt like sandpaper. Also, is your body hygiene as poor as your facial care?

It's not such an illogical association. It's generally assumed that a man gets up, brushes his teeth and showers, cleansing himself in a nice lather of soap. He washes his hair with shampoo, not bar soap. Then, he carefully and thoroughly shaves and doesn't put on too much cologne or after-shave; so the scent doesn't knock you out, clear across the room. He applies deodorant to his freshly cleansed armpits. (Applying deodorant to unclean armpits doesn't work because bacteria from the previous day multiply and you end up with body odor that is scented.) If you omit such an obvious part of this regimen, she's going to wonder about the parts she can't see.

Besides the cleanliness associations, a well-groomed face makes your wonderful smile more attractive. So, if this is not part of your daily ritual, include it. Also, it is easier to shave daily because the stubble is shorter. Shaving will be less painful and less work because stubble won't be getting stuck in the razor blade.

If you have a beard, there are a few things to consider. It is your choice whether or not to have one. However, accept the fact that some women just do not find them attractive.

A large percentage of the women I know do not like to be kissed or caressed by a hairy face with hairy lips. But, there are some, although a minority, who prefer beards and can immediately be aroused by such a kiss! The choice is yours.

Is your beard neatly trimmed? If not, you might want to reconsider your beard style. Is it hiding your smile? A barber can help you with a beard and moustache trim so we can see those soft lips. He/she can also help you choose a facial hairstyle other than a full beard, so your face is partially shaven, such as a moustache and/or sideburns or a goatee or a full beard with a sculpted perimeter.

Does your beard grow out sparse and scraggly and in different colors? You might consider shaving it off to see if you get a better social reception. You can always grow it back if you are disappointed or uncomfortable without it. Just please consider that although you will look different and perhaps feel naked at first, you will likely receive many compliments. Accept them as genuine as they likely are. They reflect that you look more appealing to women than before. Just give it a little time and the feeling of nakedness will likely fade and if you follow the rest of my advice, you may find yourself much more attractive to the opposite sex! Nice trade-off for some scraggly, sparse, facial hair, don't you think?

All done and said, there are numerous image messages you can send with your facial hair: "I'm clean and smooth," "I'm an intellectual," "I'm a musician," "I'm a hippy," or "I might have a Harley-Davidson." Just don't let it say, "I might be homeless," or "I'm a hopeless slob."

Now, let's look at the skin on your face, neck and back. Do you have acne and/or blackheads? Boy, do I have great news for you! Not only can you get effective medications like Retin A from a dermatologist, but you can also get your skin massaged, and treated by a professional! If you are on a tight budget, as most of us are, you probably can't afford a salon/spa treatment. However, you can call a beauty college for an appointment for a "facial" and/or back treatment. Let them know if you are uncomfortable being touched in that way by a man, and that you would prefer a female beautician. (Unless you would actually be more comfortable being treated by a guy.)

When you get to the beauty college, you may be asked to remove your shirt. Make sure you are clean and wearing deodorant. Next, you may lie down on a bed or a reclining chair. With soft strokes, he or she will extract your blackheads. They can also use a Tesla electronic current to zap your acne, killing the irritating bacteria, significantly reducing the redness and swelling. A facial will be very helpful if you have dry flaky skin. Get one. It feels wonderful and gives you a real positive feeling. At a beauty school, it could be free, or reasonably inexpensive, and fun!

One word of caution. **She is not your date.** *She is a professional esthetician, performing a professional service to improve your appearance so you can get a date. She may even refuse any more service if you engage in inappropriate conversation or behavior. Just lay back and enjoy a half hour of heavenly skin therapy!*

Let's move on to your hair. Is it your crowning glory or is it just a bunch of protein fibers hanging on your head? Kudos to you if your hair is clean, shiny, manageable, and well styled. Keep it up. If not, go to your barber. Try asking him or her if you would look better with another style.

If you go to the same barber, the chances are that they give the same cut over and over because you never ask for anything new. Most barbers or beauticians will be glad to offer optional hair styles that may spice up your look.

Remember, hair grows a half-inch per month, so it really shouldn't take too long to replace your old look, should nobody compliment you or if women avert their eyes. Chances are that you will get compliments. Barbers really know their head and face shapes and hair types, making them quite qualified to help you with a new look.

If you're younger, and want to be trendy and want the slightly messy "spiky look," a "unisex" shop (a salon that has both male and female clients) is the best place to go. If you live at home and must consider and obey your parents' wishes, you may not be able to have that look. In that case, go for a "fade." That is a cut that is virtually clean-shaven on the sides and gets gradually longer on top, ranging from 3/8" to an inch. This bit of longer hair on top can be moussed and spiked. It is a great compromise and will definitely keep you out of "dork" territory. Whatever style you chose, please visit your barber *monthly, to get that half-inch taken off. Then, you will always be sharp and look like you care about yourself. Women like that very much.*

The last item on your head is superfluous hair that is hair growing on or out of your ears, nose and between your eyes. Older guys usually get the ear and nose hair. Just make sure that your barber addresses your ears. Guys of all ages can get hair between their eyebrows. You can get a pair of tweezers and remove it. Just pull quickly, like removing a band-aid. The quicker the tug (in the direction the hair grows) the less pain you will feel.

Bravo! You have a handsome, marvelous, smiling head on your shoulders now. Your body should be clean. Don't forget to clean any black stuff out from under your fingernails.

Our last personal appearance question is: what are you wearing? Usually, casual dress is your best bet. A clean T-shirt in good condition and well-fitted jeans with no holes are a safe bet, although not for every occasion. Pay some attention to what the average guy is wearing. If you have the money, buy a few of the latest "in-style" outfits for yourself. If you are on a tight budget, go to second-hand shops in, or next to, an upper income neighborhood. They generally have better clothes because wealthier people wear better clothes. I have gone to such shops and bought $60.00 shirts for $10.00, $400.00 suits for $40.00 etc. Recently I bought two new pairs of Levis 501s for $3.50 each.

If you don't find treasures on the first trip, don't give up. Return frequently because there is new stuff on the rack daily. The best stuff gets bought quickly. And about plaids: never under any circumstances, mix plaids or plaids and stripes. You might as well add a clown nose. The only time you should wear plaid to meet a girl is at a country/western event. A plaid western shirt with a cowboy hat, boots, and Levis can be very hot. A regular plaid shirt just doesn't get the same response. Trust me and don't even try plaid pants unless they make a fashion comeback. I'm not saying not to ever wear them again. I have comfortable, unsightly or eccentric clothes that I only wear at home. I just change before leaving the house.

Finally, underwear. If there is any chance of intimacy, by no means wear stained undies. You might do well to try black bikini briefs. Not only do some women find them sexy, you may feel sexier wearing them, even if intimacy is not yet imminent. This may help boost your confidence.

We've covered what women generally want visually. Let's assume you've gotten your first date.

You will have to ask for a date because there aren't too many times that women will walk up to your door and beg you to go out with them. You can call her on the phone or see her in person. In any case, be pleasant, remembering that beautiful smile (yes, keep the smile even when talking over the phone), and directly ask her out. Be specific as to time, date and social event you are considering. (Lines like "Would you like to go out sometime, somewhere"... are death!) Date requests that are not clear will certainly be rejected because they are confusing.

A conversation could go something like this: Hi, Mary (or whatever her name is), this is Bob (or whatever your name is). How are you? I hope that everything is going well. What have you been doing since I saw you last? (Always wait for her to answer and then respond appropriately to her comment.) Listen, I have been looking forward to seeing the movie (or play, or concert or whatever) and I would like to have you join me. I think it will be terrific. The movie is next Friday night at 8:00. I could pick you up at about 7:30, or if you would like, we could have a bite to eat first. In that case, I would see you at about 6:45. Which is better for you? (Note that you have not asked for a yes or no answer, but to choose between two good options!) Great! I'll see you Friday.

Always be prepared to answer the question that young ladies often ask. What should she wear? This is particularly true if it is a concert or play.

Many women have two hard and fast rules on a first date. Number one, don't let him in the front door when he drops you off. Number two; never kiss on the first date. Don't let this discourage you. She has some class. This is good. When the date is over and you have taken her home, simply ask if you can call her later in the week. If she says "no," let her go. There are many available women. You must keep patiently trying until you find the one who wishes to have a relationship with you. Even neurotypical men must go on first dates with numerous women before they find a prospective partner.

On the other hand, you might find yourself on a date with a woman who is very sexually interested in you, but you have decided that she is not someone you are really interested in dating. Do you take advantage of her? Have sex with her simply for your pleasure without any caring for her feelings? The answer is easy. No! This is a very bad idea. Short-term gain, long-term pain! You are sending a false message she will, and should, take as a commitment. She may very well desire a continuing relationship with you. I know that this "easy score" can be tempting, but it is unfair and unkind to her and could be very bad news for you if she has a big brother who does not take kindly to your deceit.

Assuming that you both want a second social engagement and you are out with her having a good time, caress her hand softly and see if she caresses your hand back. Gently hold her hand and tell her how much you enjoy being with her. If she smiles and blushes, gently smile back. Allow some time for her to respond. She might not say anything. That is not necessarily a rejection.

Even if she has been talkative throughout the date, she might just be shy at this moment, but very pleased at this initial physical/romantic contact. If she is still holding hands, look at her and smile. Lift her *hand a little and kiss it. If she doesn't pull her hand away or slap you, CONGRATULATIONS! You have made it into the doorway of the magic kingdom of kissing and necking! But don't rush it. Those rather hefty doors can still eject you and slam shut in your face, and end the relationship, or damage it.*

Retain your gentlemanly, romantic demeanor, even if she begins trembling with excitement and/or breathing more heavily. If all signs are "go," proceed to a gentle kiss on the cheek. If she turns her head toward you in response, give her a soft kiss on the lips but no contact from your tongue yet. And by all means, no lip smashing kisses. Heavier lipped kisses with great pressure are reserved for moments of highly aroused passion.

If she turns her head away, it means to call it quits right here. But don't just excuse yourself and go. She will likely become highly offended and never see you again. Women almost universally require conversation before, a little during, and absolutely after, any degree of sexual encounter. After the first kiss or two is an ideal time to hold her quietly and just listen to each other breathe together. Then, with soft, full lips, kiss her on the hand, cheek or lips and tell her that you want to see more of her.   (In the unlikely event that she takes you literally, she could unbutton her shirt or pull it off completely. This happens every 100,000 dates or so!) Far more likely, she may give a socially appropriate response, such as a time, date and place for your next date.

In either case, you've got the green light to enter the "necking" phase. I suggest you gracefully but longingly end the session here if this is your first or second date. Express your desire toward her and she might also express hers. Please leave her desiring more. If you go too far, she might feel dirty and embarrassed afterward and call it quits. Don't take that chance!!

Remember, no matter how hot and steamy things get at any point in the encounters, always be a gentleman before and after. Some women want you to be a gentleman during and some want you to lose all inhibition and be a totally wild animal. You should be able to figure out which by her behavior.

Before engaging in heavy necking, which may happen on the third date or even much later, you should have a conversation about your moral and religious beliefs concerning sex. This is good for many reasons. First, it is clear that you don't want to violate any laws. Second, neither of you want the burden of a guilty conscience, and last you don't want to ruin the chances of the potential for a lasting relationship.

At this point, she may tell you directly or imply that she is a virgin. If so, she may very well be saving herself for marriage. Don't try to "make a woman out of her" in a highly aroused moment of passion. She will either loath and despise you for taking away her virtue or she will pressure you and entrap you into a marriage before you are ready. She *will feel she must reclaim her state of virtue. Generally speaking, women feel different about virginity because of social norms and pressures. But some women will gladly lose their virginity. Find out first.*

If you are a virgin, too, give pause to consider your reasons for virginity before entering into heavy petting (this is when you most easily lose your virginity). Are you a virgin because you just have not been able to "get any?" Or are you a virgin for moral reasons? In what kind of relationship do you want to lose your virginity? Serious, deep and possibly permanent, or a passing, "in-the-heat-of-the-moment" like situation? Give this serious thought, because you can only lose your virginity once.

So, if you both are on the same wavelength on interest in being sexually physical and you have both explored kissing and mutually want more. Try putting your lips to her ear and gently tongue the inside (don't get it too wet), then breathe into the ear. Not too hard, though. This should send chills of delight down her spine. If she begins breathing deeply, giggles or says "aah," continue kissing on down her neck. Bingo. You've reached the chest. See if she'll let you get your hand into her upper garment. If she says, "No," go back to speaking gently and stick to mutual kissing. Be sure to incorporate hugging and feeling her hair, face, neck, arms with your hands. Be patient about her breasts. This is a major milestone.

If she lets you slip your fingers (certainly trembling by now!) into her bra and locate her nipple, softly caress it and roll it between your fingers. Go softly and feel your senses. Notice the expressions of her senses. Is she breathing deeply? Is she pleasantly excited? Or is she tensing up and pulling your hands away?

If at this point or any other, she becomes tense or says to stop, comply. Just cool your jets. Never just plow your way through seduction just to satisfy your sexual cravings. If she says "no" and you have sex with her anyhow, that is RAPE. Even date rape will cause a judge to designate you as a sex-offender. Certainly, you do not want to start your romantic career off as a registered sex-offender.

So, what if she loves having her breast stimulated? If so, it may be the time to remove her shirt or bra. Sometimes, a woman will assist in this chore, while others may enjoy having you do it for them. Just be sensitive to her cues. If she is tensing up and grasping to keep the clothes on, stop. But continue to caress, kiss and speak gently.

If you are successful with removing the top garment, one word about the closures. Some fasten in the front while others fasten in the back. If you can't tell by feeling, just ask her. By now you are probably really ready to have a sexual intercourse. Don't rush into it yet. It takes a woman longer with more stimulation to have an orgasm, too. You will most assuredly have a quick climax once you make your penile insertion, but she won't.

If you have reached this point, now is a good time to put on your condom. (We cover this in more detail in the chapter on birth control.) No matter how urgent you feel, put that condom on!!! No ifs, ands, or buts about it. One moment of neglect can impact your life.

Now you have to remove her lower garments. You are probably going to be pretty excited at this point, but be sure to be careful to not rip clothing. Perhaps, she has assisted you in removing yours, too. If she hasn't, be sure to leave yourself as naked as she is. That way, you get the full body skin-to-skin sensation.

Now, you both should be lying down. You can gently touch her in the vaginal area for a minute or so to help her get more excited and be ready for you. Unless she has second thoughts, you are both ready to have sexual intercourse. This is the time to insert your penis. Open her legs wide enough to have your penis go between her legs. It may be more comfortable if her legs are slightly raised. Get on top and direct your penis to the middle of her vagina area. She may guide you at this point.

If she is a virgin, entry may be difficult because she has a piece of skin called a hymen, surrounded and/or partially covered by the vagina. It can range from barely obstructive to highly obstructive. Make sure she is well lubricated and don't be too forceful because for some women, it is painful to lose virginity. Some bleeding may occur but not a lot. This is normal.

Even if she is not a virgin, you probably want to go slow at first. Insertion should be a soft push until you are all the way inside of your lover. Then you can begin more rapid motions.

So you've had mutually marvelous, successful sex! Don't just close up shop. Lay there and caress. Give some more kisses. Tell her you care for her, which certainly should be true if you've gone this far! Share how happy you are. Linger together. Enjoy holding this wonderful woman.

Not every woman is going to want the same thing. These are general guidelines. You will need to find out what your woman specifically wants as you get to know her. Finally, in the case of the tactilely defensive woman: If she wants to be touched but has difficulty with it, patiently try different kinds of touch to find what works. Try soft touches. That may be painful. Try firm, sure touches. Sometimes that works better. If not, ask her what she wants you to try. Perhaps attaining a comfort level is necessary to overcoming that touch barrier. Get to know her. Be patient. Be her friend.

Things can be highly individualistic when it comes to courtship and sex. What has been outlined here is a basic how-to manual. If your partner is on the spectrum, she may have additional, varied or different needs. Please get to know them. Engage in mutual pleasures.

In conclusion, let me add that this chapter has mostly addressed what women want sexually. Let's not forget the rest of her. Hopefully, *before you reached the sexual stage you have gotten to know her as a person. What are her opinions on various subjects? What are her areas of expertise? Does she have special interests, hobbies, fantasies, goals for the future? Share them with her. Let her share yours, too. You will find she enriches your world.*

Hopefully, if you have learned all of these things, then sexual relations will be frosting on the cake and a deep, long-term relationship will blossom. Good luck!!

Birth Control, Disease Prevention and Personal Responsibility

Editor's Note: Nothing in this chapter is meant to encourage pre-marital sexual activity. It does recognize that there are those who choose that path. However, if you have someone you care for deeply and may marry, celibacy until marriage has MANY benefits. As you read this chapter, you will see that very few of these negatives apply to celibate individuals or those in a committed relationship.

Sex is not an activity that can be enjoyed without regard for the consequences. Sure, it is easy to get hot, steamy, and urgent. You carelessly and irresponsibly forego the condom. But what else has happened? Is there a baby now? Are you disease free? Surely you've heard lots of condom talk by now. But the pregnancy and out of wedlock statistics (900,000 teenage pregnancies per year, over half a million babies born out of wedlock) tell us that many people are ignoring birth control!

Guys, listen up. Girls don't just get pregnant. They don't get pregnant from reading dirty magazines, watching *Sex in The City*, or by using the wrong public toilet, either. Girls need someone like you to "help" them get pregnant, someone who may care more about his momentary pleasure than he does about hygiene or pregnancy prevention. Guys don't have as much freedom to be irresponsible, as their Dads might have had. Back in my generation, when a woman took a man to court to prove he was the father, she would often wind up defending her reputation against a room full of her "lover's" fraternity brothers, all willing to claim (commit perjury) that they had sex with her. Thanks to modern science, those days are gone!

No longer is it solely the mother who is stuck with the entire burden of parenting an unplanned-for child. DNA tests can irrefutably prove fatherhood. The courts can order maintenance (child support) payments from the father. If the mother has to go on welfare, Human Resources Agencies aggressively pursue you for payment. You can end up in jail if you can't or don't pay. You might not even have visitation rights for your child! Birth control is equally the man's responsibility!

I know, my wife is really bumming you guys out with this. When you are young, a lot of you don't want to hear this. You have been brainwashed by MTV, *Playboy*, and all of the other mind-rot. You may even be stupid enough to think that women are just sexual furniture for your enjoyment. But they are not!

Some may ask, "Why doesn't the woman 'just' get an abortion?" Well, for one thing, this baby in progress is in her body, not yours. It is her right to decide (Girls, if you know that your lover is about to practice unsafe sex, it is your right and responsibility to say "no.")

Guys, imagine yourself with a possible baby inside of you, something that most women want to eventually experience in the right situation. Do you want to have some doctor cut into you and stop that? An abortion is no easy experience for any woman who has it. If you care about your lovers, you won't put them into such a situation.

So let's get to know condoms. Your condom is your friend. It'll keep you safe and out of a lifetime of trouble. First, let's shop for some before you need them. You should do your best to select the right size. Buy one that appears large enough, take it home and try it on. You don't want to wait until the critical minute just before sex, to fumble with it and realize it doesn't fit well! If it fits, fine. But don't use that trial condom. Toss it away and buy a few of the same size or a size smaller or larger if it didn't fit.

Proper condom use requires lubrication. To lubricate the condom, you should buy K-Y Jelly®. It is a very good, very pleasurable lubricant for the woman, too. Put a little bit in the tip of the condom. This will give you a more natural feel, so pleasure is not so dramatically decreased. Don't put too much in, because you don't want to lubricate the inside so much that the condom slips off.

Men should take responsibility for the condom. Although a woman might carry some in her purse, she doesn't necessarily know what size fits best and feels best for the male. If you are sexually active, the condom is your best line of defense against disease, although it is not totally effective. Condoms can slip off, leak or break. Therefore, pregnancy can happen, too. Even with a condom regularly used, the woman really should use the pill. If she is using a birth control pill, the condom should still be used because there might be days when the pill is forgotten.

(However, if you do have sex with only a condom for protection, remember what a prominent doctor said, "We have a name for folks who use only condoms for birth control - parents!)

And if a pregnancy results, you, the male, are still responsible! The sad truth is that no matter how conscientiously you follow all of the advice we give, the only totally risk free alternative is to not have sex at all.

If you have a problem with the idea of using a condom, we hope this chapter has helped you accept the need for using them. If you are entering into a monogamous relationship, you may feel that a condom is not needed. But you both need to never violate the monogamous vow. You should go together to see a doctor to get a clean bill of health and birth control counseling. Never slip up on birth control unless you are ready to take the very important step of meeting the awesome responsibility of becoming parents.

For some people in our community, birth control is not an option. The decision is taken out of their hands by parents who have a girl with autism sterilized. Sometimes, the person doesn't even know what has been done at the time. It is usually done without her consent. I think this is wrong, period. I know a number of autistic women, including Mary, who are great mothers and a good number of normal women who are lousy mothers. I see no logical argument for sterilization. Name one person born, and either put up for adoption or raised in an orphanage, who would not have wished to live at all.

Jerry and I disagree on this. I do think it may be wise to sterilize an autistic woman who appears to lack potential to rear or be responsible for a baby. There are way too many single mothers as it is. This is a very difficult situation even for mothers who are not challenged by autism. The woman's family, who does not want the child to be adopted, may unfairly carry the potential burden.

In another chapter we discuss the merits of celibacy. That is about as sure a method of birth control as you can find. However, there are other methods of birth control besides abstinence that are totally effective. The downside is that neither of them can be practiced with complete assurance that the person can reverse the process later if they decide that they do want to become a parent.

The male operation is a vasectomy. It is a simple, inexpensive operation in which a surgeon ties off a pair of tubes in the scrotum. Effectively shutting off the vas deferens tubes, through which sperm flows from the testicles out into the seminal vesicle.   This operation is cheaper, safer and less complicated than the female equivalent.

I know. I had one in 1982. There is some swelling after the procedure, but I was walking and working, driving a taxi, a day after the operation. The operation prevents sperm from leaving the penis and entering a woman's vagina. No sperm, no babies!

Reversing a vasectomy is more expensive. Recent costs are between $6,000.00 and $10,000.00 for a reversal attempt. Even after that, there is a recovery period before one can begin sex safely again and the chance of fatherhood is only forty to sixty percent. If you are thinking about having a vasectomy, ask yourself, are you willing to accept the probability that you will never be able to be a father?

The female operation, called a tubal ligation, is irreversible. No ifs, ands or buts. So ladies, please think about this. Maybe you think this will mean lots of fun, safe sex at twenty. However, you won't be twenty forever. What if you meet a really great partner who wants to be a father, after you've had your fill of life in the fast lane? The tubal ligation is not an easy solution. If you have it, you need to accept the consequences. On the other hand, for women who have had children and simply want no more, this is a final answer.

The tubal ligation is an operation in which the fallopian tubes, which carry the eggs from the ovaries to the uterus, are sealed. That is, a tiny spark of electricity burns the end of the tube and it is sealed shut permanently. Eggs can no longer enter the uterus. If you don't want any more babies, or you absolutely never want to have a baby, this is the operation for you.

Another surgical procedure for females is the IUD, the Intrauterine Device. The IUD is a reliable method for preventing pregnancy for a long time. It is inserted into a woman's uterus, during the time of menstruation, at a qualified doctor's office. There are two kinds available. The progestocet IUD must be replaced yearly. The copper-T IUD is effective for up to ten years. These are safe, time-tested methods, but availability of these and any other birth control procedures may change in your area, depending on the political climate. You must never have such a procedure done illegally. You can die if an unqualified person does this.

There are other methods of contraception used by females. A woman who plans to be sexually active should visit an office of Planned Parenthood and thoroughly explore all options available. Be sure to ask about diaphragms, spermicides and the "morning after pill." I advise the reader to go to the office of professionals who can explain these choices thoroughly. The perceived level of risk and/or inconvenience will depend on the woman and there is not enough space here to describe all birth control options in sufficient detail.

I hope that readers, by now, will appreciate how much simpler, safer and cheaper your life will be if you practice some form of safe sex; an operation, abstinence, condoms, will all work if you just use some common sense and care about your future and that of your lover.

There is more "fun" ahead. Birth control is only one of your concerns. Sex also means the risk of contracting a variety of venereal diseases. A venereal disease is one that is transmitted through sexual activity. Some venereal diseases are also transmitted by other methods. These diseases can be transmitted by almost any kind of sexual contact, but usually result in discomfort, pain and embarrassment.

However, that is not the case with AIDS. I think you all know how deadly AIDS is. I used to work as a delivery man for a pharmacy. Some of our regular customers were people with AIDS. None of them are alive today to read this book. It was very sad to watch such nice people deteriorate, despite the best medication available. Everything we have mentioned in terms of condom use and general hygiene will help you avoid such a fate.

But if you have a new partner, you can never be too safe! You can both get a free AIDS test and make sure that you don't have it. If either of you are diagnosed with the disease, you are aware of your challenge. Then, you and your partner can accept the risk or not. If you have it and don't tell a partner, that is simply unethical and in many parts of the country, illegal. If you don't know you have it and you infect someone who fares even worse with it than you do, you will feel horrible. So, if you have ever had a sexual relationship with a person with whom you were not absolutely 100% committed, or if you ever did illegal drugs at all, please get the free AIDS test. We did.

In Hollywood there was a gay-lesbian health clinic that gave free tests. We aren't gay or lesbian, but their services were available to anyone, and there should be similar services in your city. Look in the yellow pages or call Planned Parenthood.

The test is not totally accurate. There is a small chance that you may have AIDS, and it will not be detected. Or you may have a test result that says you have AIDS when you don't. In this case, try another test or two and see what happens. If you don't have it, the majority of tests should come out negative. As important as testing is, it is not the only thing you need to do to combat AIDS and other sexually transmitted diseases. You need to look at your lifestyle and see if you are putting yourself at risk.

What do I mean by that? Some diseases are also transmitted by use of a common needle. I hope you are not using heroin or other injected drugs. If you are, get a grip and stop! At least don't share needles with other users. You can also get AIDS from contact with the blood from an open wound of someone who has AIDS. The best way to avoid AIDS is to avoid any sexual contact with people whose lifestyles put themselves at risk for it - gays, heroin users or other addicts who injected drugs. Finally, **never** receive an injection except those given by a licensed medical professional.

There isn't enough space here to list and describe all of the little "treats" that you may result from sexual activity, in the way of unwanted diseases. Be smart. If you experience anything unusual, such as pain in urination, a sore on or near a genital area or other symptom, go to a doctor and have this examined.

If you don't have a regular doctor or medical insurance, your city or county should have a clinic available, usually for free. Society places a high premium on preventing the spread of these diseases. The earlier you detect them, the better. To help those who help you, it is advisable to share with them the names of recent sexual partners, although this is not legally necessary. The most important thing is to make sure of your own health.

We hope this chapter has not been depressing. The good news is that most people can go through life, have a sexually satisfying life and never wind up in the situations we have tried to help you avoid. Unwanted pregnancies, abortions, and diseases are important issues. You have the knowledge to make wise choices in your life. The choice is up to you.

" I took the one less traveled by, and
that has made all of the difference."
— **Robert Frost**

Roads Less Traveled by and the
Right to Travel Them

*Editor's Note: Nothing in this chapter should be taken as
an endorsement of any alternative lifestyle. We respect the
rights of the individual and those who love and care for them
to make decisions that are in the best interest of all concerned.*

By the time most of you reach adulthood, you will have
endured many different attempts to ram a naturally round peg
(you) into the square peg of normalcy. Most of these efforts come
from well-meaning people. In your presence, they may have talked
about you to doctors and other "experts," as if you were not even
in the room. Sometimes it is hard to believe that they love and
respect you, but the truth is that they just don't know any better.
They sincerely believe that being and acting as close to normal as
possible represents the best chance for you to have a happy life.
Often they are prisoners of their own insecurity. Their self-image is
often a product of how they feel others perceive them. Many of
us, on the other hand, hear a different drummer and are not as
concerned about the perceptions of other people. The truth may

be that we could stand being a little more concerned of the views of others and our parents a little less.

The bottom line is this: no matter how heroic, dedicated and wonderful people may have been on your behalf, you don't owe them any more than your best effort in return. You have to find social and sexual happiness in the way that you really want it. To live a lie and be what others want you to be is an insult to you, everyone who cares about you, and to whatever Great Force created all of us.

The point of this chapter is that the drum that beats in your life's parade may not be the same drum that beats for the life parades of other people. You may not want a conventional sexual or social lifestyle. There are other ways to be happy. By the time we on the spectrum become adults, all but the most strident people understand that "normalcy" may never be an option.

You can have a life, and that life can be different. Yet it can be as happy, productive and fulfilling as you want. But you have to stop disliking yourself for not being the person everyone else wants. Meaning well, many times parents try very hard and waste a lot of money trying to get you to be a different person. Many times the line between improvement and molding you to be something you cannot be is very thin.

I hope that your family and friends support you if you decide to socially go against the social flow. My parents would have. They were conservative, but tolerant. I remember them discussing an interesting movie, *Guess Who's Coming to Dinner*, starring Poitier, Tracy, and Hepburn. The movie portrayed a black man being introduced to his white future in-laws. My parents didn't know anyone in such a fix, but they agreed that it could happen and that it should be allowed to happen. That made me feel comfortable. I always knew that what made me happy would make them happy. Not everyone is so lucky.

It saddens me to see a minority of our parents be so rigid in their beliefs that there is little room for deviation. Often, they will write a check for any amount, but not have time for a minute's worth of listening.

It takes an exceptional amount of flexible structure and tolerance to raise any child. I will never be a father and I was too judgmental to be a good stepfather when I had even half a chance. If intolerance reigns, no child's self-image will survive, normal or not. If your parents are this way, about all you can do is hope they wake up and understand your perceptions of the world. Maybe a good starting point is to have them read this chapter!

Perhaps you find that life requires too much constant changing and juggling of your attention span. You might seek a lifestyle that has more order, minimizes the social stress, or in some other way relieves the major stress you feel because of the way your autism affects you.

Obviously, the social and sexual arena is a challenge. You have the option of trying to join in the social crowd and try to make your feelings and attitudes fit in with the mainstream. However, this may not be the path for you, and you may seek other options.

Maybe the most obvious alternative is celibacy. Celibacy, abstaining from sexual interaction, has some advantages. You don't have to worry about unwanted pregnancy or sexually transmitted diseases. Considering the carelessness of today, those are important advantages.

Celibacy also removes the challenge of juggling career focus with the emotional complications introduced by romance. I think that is how some adults like Temple Grandin have used celibacy to an advantage. They seek fulfillment in a career that others look for in relationships. Celibacy may work better for those at the top of the IQ spectrum. I am not so sure it will work as well for the rest of us.

Celibacy was my choice for a decade, with the exception of a date rape: I said, "No." He said, "Yes." That was the end of that. When he was through, I felt sick to my stomach. Many boys are simply stronger

than girls, and girls can get bullied or beat into a sexual encounter.
This is why girls have to be careful and boys have to be aware of their
strength and not abuse girls with it.

It wasn't until after I turned thirty-eight that a romance seemed to
blossom. We dated. I consented to sex. He cast me off in a matter of
a few months. Used again! I was livid and had a nervous breakdown.
My "second virginity" was lost in what I viewed as another sexual
exploitation. I had been saving myself for "the one" and now I had to
search for another "one."

(That was when I called the autism society in San Gabriel Valley,
seeking help for my sensitive but volatile autistic self. I was referred to
an adult support group, AGUA, and given Jerry's phone number. **Jerry**
may not fully realize this, but even though I was a mother of
two grown sons when we met, he is my first and last actual
romantic relationship.)

If a celibate person really wants to be that way (a big if), he or
she can still go out with friends who accept this, and have just as
much fun, dancing, throwing darts, etc. just like anyone else. What
happens at the end of the evening should be a private affair.

This is similar to how some people react to seeing a wedding
or engagement ring on a finger. That will discourage most people,
but it will turn others into absolute predators. They have no feel-

ing for the target, whether celibate, engaged, or married. Their ego just wants a conquest, so they can brag about breaking the barrier, "converting the nun," or "having the last piece of cake before the wedding."

This is especially true for celibate women. Sometimes men, usually those of low character or self-esteem, view celibacy as a challenge to be met in any way they can. My advice to any woman choosing celibacy is to be careful.

Celibacy can be a permanent, life-long decision or one you make for a period of time. For example, you could choose to remain celibate until you marry. It can also be seen as a temporary respite from social stresses caused by sexual activity. Many people, myself included, have been celibate for a while after a divorce, being widowed or otherwise ending a long-term monogamous relationship. In any case, it is not a good idea to plunge right away into another relationship when one ends that meant a lot to you.

I have also benefited from just telling myself that I was not looking for sex or relationships. When I went to social gatherings, I was there just to have fun, with no expectations. That isn't quite the same as celibacy, but it has a similar effect. Without the pressure to impress or perform, I find myself more at ease. I was in such a state of mind when I met Mary.

Celibacy, therefore, has definite advantages if assumed with proper awareness of how others will react to your lifestyle. It probably has a better chance of success if you get a lot of fulfillment from a career or an intense personal hobby that you love to do, alone or not. I don't think it will ever work if it is not what you really want to do. There are other social paths beyond celibacy.

Some autistic people, I believe, choose an **alternative** social lifestyle. In other words, they are homosexuals, otherwise known as gays or lesbians. In effect, they choose to have a sexual relationship with someone of their own sex. Some of these people know from an early age that this is their desire, but I believe that others decide to go that way later on. In any event, I think that the important thing here is whether it is really what one wants to do. If it is, then other than advising them to practice safe sex, which all of us should do, what is the big deal? It's often only a big deal to a parent or "friend" who is more concerned about the "damage" to his image or reputation than he is about the happiness of his child or friend.

One interesting factor here is that a relationship is a relationship is a relationship. It takes as many social skills to have a gay relationship as it does a heterosexual one. Both ways can bring acceptance and enjoyment; both can cause strife and concern. If you or your loved one chooses an alternative lifestyle, it can bring many of the same challenges as a normal relationship. You can have argu-

131

ments about many of the same things as a heterosexual couple, finances, colors of furniture, times for meals, etc.

(I realize that a homosexual relationship is rarely the first choice parents have for their child. Honestly, everything being equal, it would not be my choice either. However, wouldn't you want your child to be happy in a homosexual relationship rather than being alone and miserable?)

You may find members of your own sex appealing sexually. If so, then be relaxed with your decision and get on with your life. Don't make being gay a crusade like Ellen DeGeneres did. Her TV ratings didn't tank because she "came out" (publicly revealed her status). In my opinion, the show died because she turned it into a crusade for gay living, period. Fine. You're gay. I'm happy. My cat is depressed. Get a life.

However, in the case of a homosexual relationship, sometimes a man or woman with a low self-image may endure incredible abuse from a dominant gay or lesbian partner. If it is the first relationship of any kind, the security of a relationship that is miserable can be less scary than a return to social isolation. (That can also happen, and too often does, in straight relationships.)

To those of you who chose sexual experimentation, remember: It is your decision to try it and by the same token, your right to back out of it. And as for trying an alternative sexual orientation, I have to tell you that some who try it wind up as miserable as they were before.

Another option, although it does not exactly qualify as sexual, is the option of joining a cult. This is something that our people sometimes consider because of the lure of being in something that is orderly, takes all decisions out of your hands and usually preys on the lack of self-esteem by telling the individual that they will be loved by all other members. This is NOT a healthy choice. It represents a threat to the person they recruit and the family which is usually estranged from their son or daughter. If any of you are considering this option, please, please don't. Talk to your parents, friends, and other support members, about this path that can ruin your life and that of your parents.

It's time to step back and look at all of these alternatives. I don't necessarily promote any of them. The question I pose is this: Who is to say what is the right path to happiness? If some of these alternatives are acceptable to "normals," then our people have the right to seek them too. Except of course the invitation to join a cult, bad move, friend!

This was a somewhat difficult chapter to write. However, I have lived longer than most readers and believe my experience and perspectives may help many of you. Thanks to the social exposure afforded by years of taxi driving, I have had my eyes opened to ways of living that I never would have considered for myself. Literally, I have seen everything, including heroin addicts shoot up in my back seat. (I haven't covered drugs, because it is not directly related to sex, but that is a sure loser, I can assure you.) I know much of this chapter is not what some people wanted to read about.

We all get but one life. There is no one set way to live that everyone can strive for and find happiness by achieving. If we truly love ourselves, our children, friends and neighbors, we must love them for their courageous efforts to live as they are meant to live, taking risks doing so.

Rape, Molestation and Abuse

We auties and aspies are prime targets for abuse. There are many degrees of sexual molestation, ranging from being mocked or teased about penis size in the locker room or lack of social activity to being anally or vaginally raped at any age.

Sex is supposed to be a "magical" event that came along with the most beautiful, blissful love in life. But some jerk could come along and take it away! If this happens, you have to be careful to not let his ignorance and crime ruin your life. Remember, that the bad acts of others cannot make you bad. It is often difficult to rise above the actions of a bad person, but your future depends on your understanding that you are far better than the sick person who took advantage of you.

I have some good news for you! You still can look forward to the first time you have sex with love! It'll be heavenly. This kind of sex is "lovemaking." It leaves a couple with profound feelings of happiness, satisfaction, and connectivity.

If you are a victim, you must first come to terms with what happened to you. You are not dirty. Even if you were seduced or it simply was not your sexual preference. This could leave you with confused feelings about your sexuality. Some rapes are clearly defined. You are physically forced to do something despite protests and resistance. It hurts. You hate and revile your attacker. It may even be someone you know, and too many times it is someone you trusted.

The truth is that the far bigger crime and injury is the taking away of trust and innocence, rather than the physical injury. This is where the support of love ones can play such a big part. If any of these negatives happen to you; their love, caring and positive comments are the most important medicines a victim can ever have.

I am lucky that this is not in my history, but I know peers who are not so lucky. (As we said in our introduction, this injury happened to Mary and she did not have the family support that could have been so helpful.) It is not easy when the attacker is someone close to you, neighbor, relative, "friend," date, etc. However, you can still get help. You can report that person, even a family member, to authorities. The sooner you report it, the better. It is difficult to punish the offender when years pass after the offense. Besides, the offender is likely to find another family member, babysitter or other victim once he is tired of molesting you.

We have a word of caution to parents and siblings of a nonverbal child. You have to be really careful about information coming through alternative communication, also known as facilitated communication (FC). This is where a non-verbal person has a facilitator hold their arm or shoulder while they type out messages. We have known fathers to be ordered away from their child for many months over activities that never happened except in the mind of the individual or the facilitator. This doesn't mean that accusations should not be taken seriously, but collaborating evidence needs to be found.

There is serious controversy over whether FC is reliable when a person's hand is physically in contact with the facilitator's hand. There have even been reports that typing can be manipulated even if there is only light contact at the shoulder or elbow. Some people have started with FC and progressed to completely reliable, independent typing. So FC can't be tossed out. But if FC is used in your home or at school, you must be careful about the character of the facilitator.

Speaking about facilitators, and in fact anyone who works with your child, you should have them checked out carefully including a background check and a fingerprint record. Your youngster is far too valuable to take any chances.

Whether the victim is verbal or not, most abuse and rape cases are very apparent misuse of power. However, some rapes are less clearly defined because they involve seduction. You start out saying "no" but the person persists. You cave in and allow sex to happen. This is not classic rape and not often enforceable in the courts if you accede to the seduction. However, it is still a misuse of power to achieve an end and you need to rely on your instincts. If you don't want to have sex, don't do it. Say "no," loud and clear.

I must say that in retrospect, I feel somewhat guilty of this, myself. If you look at the subject of sexual rights with a clear head, you realize that if you force your sexual will on a partner, it is not a healthy relationship or a fair one. Depending on how much "encouragement" is used, it could easily be viewed as rape in the eyes of the woman, and the judge!

All forms of rape can lead to feelings of guilt, filth, insecurity and anger on the part of the woman. It is most advisable to see a sex therapist if you have been raped at any age. A professional can help you work through your feelings and understand the dynamics of the situation. If a rape or exploitation is still going on, it can be stopped. Hopefully, your parents will be a safe harbor for you and will give you comfort.

There are also rape counseling centers. Look in your phone book. I found that my county government pages listed a child abuse hot line (if you are under eighteen) and an adult abuse hot line. In the white business pages, I found the rape crisis center. In the yellow pages, under rape services, it said, "See crisis intervention, human services organizations, information services, social service organizations, support groups, women's organizations." It may not be in that exact form, but you can find help in your phone directory.

If you are in a small town, such services might not exist. You may need to make a trip to the city to get rape counseling services. By all means, make the effort.

If you've never been raped, you want to make sure that you never are. Your chances of rape, or over-seduction and/or sexual exploitation are greatly increased when you start dating. That is no reason to not date, only to be aware and to follow some simple rules.

Don't let your date in to your apartment or home until you feel safe doing so. You can have a good night kiss in front of your door. You are a lot safer there and it gives you a good chance to see how much of gentleman he really is. Also, as we said in another chapter, nothing is lost with a little peck on the cheek or a slight hug on the first date. If he is a decent guy, he will respect you more for having some class and be back for another date.

A place where it is easy to get molested is in the car. If you want to park and kiss, stay in the front seat. Getting into the back seat makes you much more vulnerable and gives a signal to almost any guy that you are willing to go further sexually. If you don't intend to go all the way, stay in the front seat. Keep your boundaries well defined. Stop activity the very minute you feel uncomfortable!

If you are in the car with your date and he begins driving somewhere other than where you have agreed to go, get him to stop at a convenience store. Tell him you need a coke or something. Get out at a red light if you must. Call a taxi, call a friend to pick you up or take a bus home.

Never go on a date without some emergency money!

Never let anyone make you feel obligated to go any further than you want. A fuzzy area of rape is when you do agree to go "all the way" and the other person wants you to perform acts that you find gross or distasteful. If you don't like it, don't do it. Don't let them force you to do it. If this ruins it for the other person, that is their problem, not yours.

Never allow any form of sexual activity that you do not really want to do. If your self-image is poor, you might not stop him/her because you are afraid that you will never get a date with that person again if you resist. Hellooo! Those who force themselves on victims are not the types that form relationships. Maybe at "best" you'll get a few more "date rapes" out of this person, then he is on to the next victim.

There are places and jobs that are potentially dangerous for us. One is in a group home. We find that group homes are often staffed by underpaid people, who have not received adequate background checks. As we have said before, be sure all staff have been finger-printed and had background checks. The supervisor of the home should be willing to offer records that will assure that the proper checks have been made. The risk factor is particularly high if the autistic person is nonverbal. He or she is not able to defend himself by shouting and getting someone's attention.

Schools or offices after hours can be dangerous. It is nice to stay after school and help the teacher or other administrators, but sure you are not alone with someone unless it is absolutely neces-sary and, if so, follow some of the other safety procedures we list a little later.

Some jobs expose us to potential abuse. These are jobs in which we are isolated and vulnerable to a dominating co-worker or manager. Custodial and office work where we are alone, night security jobs, evening shifts at hospitals where there are not many people around, etc. In these situations, be sure to carry a can of mace or some other self-defense mechanism. If you can afford it, a cellular phone is a good idea. They can be programmed to call a number like the police or home by just touching one button. Also, always be aware of the location of the closest exit or person who can help in the event you need assistance.

Other jobs expose our social naivete to predators. For example, I was a taxi driver at night. Occasionally, I had fares in my taxi, gay men, who tried to make advances on me, touching me or saying provocative things. Usually, I just had to say that I was not interested, but on a couple of times, I had to knock some jerk on the head to discourage his paws from touching me.

Delivery jobs such as pizza delivery can expose you to some real perverts as well. It is best not to enter an apartment if you deliver food. You may not get out safely. Just bring the item to the door and tell the person that you are not allowed to enter apartments. Take the money and go safely. I remember when Mary and I delivered pizzas, there was a fellow with designs on her. He would specifically call our store and ask for Mary to deliver the pizza. Mary was not comfortable with this creep. The next time he called, I delivered the pizza instead. His response: "Where's the chick?" My response: "You mean, my roommate?" I think that shut him up for good. It is important to remember that no company can legally require you to endanger yourself in order to deliver a product. Unfortunately, the owner of our restaurant was a pig with less sensitivity than a pet rock. He was a slob who couldn't keep his hands off his employees. From my experience in the restaurant field, this seems to be a common problem. Mary and I quit to avoid that kind of abuse, but no job is worth keeping if your employer can't understand your right to sexual safety.

One good thing to do, and for many reasons, is for you to take some self-defense classes. First, they make you safer, and second, they will help you to be in better shape. Usually you lose weight, gain confidence, and have an overall better attitude.

We can't cover every possibility for rape, molestation and sexual abuse. Our point is that we are targets, and we, our parents and caregivers, need to be aware of our increased danger and to take steps to reduce the likelihood that it will happen.

This is a very unfortunate fact of life. If it does happen that you are abused or raped, the important thing to remember is that you have done nothing wrong and have every right to go on and have a happy relationship with anyone else you choose to bring into your life.

But better than having to recover from an attack is to take steps to prevent it from happening. I hope that we have given some ideas that will help you to be safer.

What About the Late Bloomers?

Socializing, Careers and the Internet -what a combination!

Most autistic people will be late bloomers socially. Some women may get early sexual experience, but it is rarely healthy or social in nature. The term, "late bloomer" is a relative term here. A normal late bloomer may have his first date at eighteen. Many on the spectrum may not have their first date until well into their twenties, or even older. Even though a woman may naively be led into sex, she may not get any proper opportunity for commensurate social growth until years later. She is, overall still a late bloomer, sex or not. The question we pose is: Is it ever too late for our people? More importantly, how can we give our late-starting people a real chance, those who want it, to find partners and sexual happiness and fulfillment?

The answer to that requires a dramatic shift in the priorities of the autism community. As long as I have been involved in autism, since 1989, our focus has been on needs of young children, some of us seeking "cures." Although more needs to be done, particularly on the social level, there has been real progress for younger children. But we who are affected will all one day become adults. For most of us, the effects of autism will still be more than subtle. Our community must understand that the cute five-year-old child of today will live to be 15, 25, 35, 45, 55 and beyond. The needs will change with age. They will always have needs and they will be just as important as the needs of any autistic poster child.

Is there hope for late bloomers? Absolutely! I didn't marry until I was forty-six, and that was after going years without even a date, before I met my future wife. A couple of my friends were first married when even older. One marriage lasted and one didn't. But the divorced man still values the experience. There is no hope without accepting risk.

Our late bloomers will need a lifetime support strategy that addresses their needs to grow, learn more skills, find work and keep surpassing barriers, including social barriers, at any age. Your child or adult always has potential and will not fail or succeed on "schedule" or become another social statistic.

Much of our growth will depend on the kind of living situation and lifetime understanding and support that we receive. I have seen both extremes. Let me say that, in some cases, where family financial resources are very limited, it may not be fair for society to expect any family to permanently house and support an autistic person who is not capable of gaining any independence.

This brings me to the subject of careers. That may seem on the surface as if it has nothing to do with sexual interest. However, any person who can find a position in society in terms of a career or satisfying job, will be far more likely to be successful in finding a relationship that is rewarding, personally and socially.

One possibility that may seem strange at first is the Merchant Marine. The Merchant Marine is a career in which one can travel a lot, getting to see interesting places. You spend much of your time on a commercial vessel. Although you are part of a team, you do spend a lot of time alone. A person may find more happiness in such a lifestyle than in any relationship. Your happiness is what counts. I have a good friend who is autistic and photographed much of our world while a merchant marine. He left that job and eventually married, but that profession was great and very interesting for a while. It probably made him more interesting and marriageable!

Another is the military. Many of our people, both male and female like the structure, pace and uniformity offered by the military. Another could be religion. Again structured, and offers the solace and peace that many of us find so appealing.

Obviously, the computer world offers great potential. Many of our peers not only work in this field but are well respected and valued in the computer world. This field values organization and reliability, very often requires less people skills than other occupations, and the pay is excellent.

How about libraries? Again, great structure and the opportunity to learn are obviously there. Many folks I know who went to work in libraries fell in love with the Dewey Decimal System! An interesting thing about this job and many that we are supremely qualified for is that they are often boring to other people. To us, the repetitive factor is often calming and satisfying whereas "normal" folks are ready to climb the walls.

Then there is the subject of where he or she will live. Some may never have to leave the home, if the plan is for them to inherit it once parents are gone. In this case, people who will be the new support should be introduced to the individual with autism early and often. The point of all of this, regarding our topic, is that autistic people need a life-plan, not a plan that loses interest after the first two decades pass and the "cure" has not been found. This plan should include social growth and encouragement.

Group homes are appealing for many families, but unfortunately there are very few in comparison to the many people who want to live there. You have to get your reservation in early and be prepared to meet the financial responsibility with either private funds or find some measure of government funding.

However, it is sometimes surprising how often a good living situation can be worked out with two or three high functioning people sharing a home. An example would be the son of the President of Future Horizons, Alex Gilpin. He shares a town house with his friend, Scott, with minimal support from TEACCH. They have someone who comes to visit about once every ten days or so to plan meals, discuss any possible problems, etc. They do their own shopping, cooking, cleaning and other household responsibilities. Both have jobs that basically meet their ongoing expenses. The neat thing about these two is that when each was twelve, this arrangement would have been thought to be a dream.

An adult on the spectrum must grow in social awareness, experience and confidence or he can stagnate. It all depends on the attitude of those around him. In too many instances, I have seen parents place a son or daughter in a setting and then expect that to be their place for their rest of their lives. That is ridiculous. Why would we expect a normal person to happily spend the rest of his life in the same general situation? People grow, move, try things, take chances, fail, win, lose, love, divorce and go through lots of changes. They may not like many of those changes and others will be voluntary. Our people don't want to spend all sixty or more years of adult life in the first situation they go into when they leave home! Even our people don't resist all change. Most of us change our clothes, too!

What often accompanies an unrealistic hope for a permanent resolution is an attitude that "someone else can worry." In a sense, that has to be allowed. Some familial burnout is only natural.

Burnout can heal with time. But desertion is never healthy for family or the autistic person. The best situations are those in which families and friends continue to be a part of an autistic person's life as other people come in to provide support formerly found in the natural home. They often need help to accomplish this.

What does all this have to do with sexual potential? Everything. One can become sexually active at ages much later than usual. The continued support and encouragement of others is very important. It helps us feel more loved and secure, which makes us more attractive.

Many young adults meet each other at places that cultivate a common interest. These should not be "negative" sites such as nightclubs, which are notoriously socially threatening environments for our people. Places like a bookstore that features poetry readings, health clubs, yoga clubs, running groups, chess clubs, or any interest group are a good bet for our people, who have little problem expressing an interest in certain subjects. In these places, our intense interest, which may not be appreciated ordinarily, might even come to a social advantage. For example, a young woman who has nervously read her first poem to a local reading club might be very flattered by the interest of an autistic man who heard it. I know that, as awkward as I may seem to the layman, I am happiest, most comfortable and most attractive, when engrossed in my passions.

There is no guarantee that any of this will ever work for some people. But the more ominous guarantee is that the most miserable members of my community are the ones whose natural support systems dry up, and they stop looking for new inspirations, activities, and interests.

There are many good reasons to have a job. Taking a position in order to use the office as a "dating pool," is NOT one of them. It is true that many relationships are started in the workplace. However, your reason for working is to accomplish something with pride, earn a living and while doing those, you can increase your skills in listening, consideration, and cooperation. All of which enhance social success.

Many of you will have to learn some skills prior to getting a good job. Typical colleges may not be the best places for many of our people to learn meaningful work skills. The best option for many may be a training program aimed toward a specific career. My wife has had three experiences in these endeavors.

I entered the University of Arizona as a music major and studied for two years. It was very enjoyable. However, I wanted to have a concrete job possibility. That is not always something that comes with a college degree. This was of great importance to me because I had two young sons and valued my independence. My first professional apprenticeship was in piano tuning and repair. I left the university after two years and studied with a good piano dealership in Tucson. My training led me to years of good-paying, interesting work in different cities, including New York, where I tuned pianos at Radio City, Apollo Theater, and for various radio stations. The advent of electronically tuned instruments reduced my income potential, and I went into other work. But I did not give up the idea of apprenticeship for a specific job, which is very practical and focused for our autistic population.

I also apprenticed in gemology, but the social climate of the gem business was not supportive of my type of people. It is important, in considering an apprenticeship; to be sure that job prospects, work conditions, and employer attitudes will be a good match for an autistic person. In gemology they were not. Fortunately, I am now in my third apprenticed career, cosmetology. This time, I found a school, mostly funded by government job-training grants, with an excellent pass rate on the state exam and a high percentage of working graduates. I had two job offers before I finished the ten-month course. I passed the state cosmetology license exam on the first try, had a license and was working within a week. I am still there.

Mary has learned far more from her various careers than just the job tasks. She gained a sense of independence that made her more able to handle social experiences as they came throughout her life. Education of one form or another should be part of everyone's life after public school. It need not be directed, initially, at a degree or job. There is much to be said for learning just because

you like to know more about something, and to not have it directed to a career.

Also, getting into classes on a subject that interests you not only
opens you to information, but also another opportunity to meet
new people. Any positive experience helps us improve our ability
to interact socially.

There are other possibilities for communication and learning,
thanks to modern technology. The Internet hosts many "lists" that
have listings of job opportunities.

However, if you are a parent, it is wise to monitor this activity.
Our people can be naïve about the offerings on the "net" and may
respond to financial opportunities that are a sham.

Many of my fellow late bloomers feel that the Internet is a good
place to find dating opportunities. As far as getting dates from the
Internet, I don't see it. However, it can be a great source of support. Many of the people with whom I trade e-mail feel that the
Internet has ended the isolation they felt, the feeling as if nobody
knew of or cared about their take on the world. That is a big
improvement!

As you grow older and do not find sufficient social opportunities in your community, many of us turn to the Internet's countless

"chat groups." They offer our people a chance to share their inter-ests in a sea of possibilities beyond autism. It is more comfortable for many of us then spontaneous personal contact for several rea-sons: You don't have to respond to any message unless you choose to and you can respond when it is convenient for you. The Internet does not interrupt your day like a telephone and demand your attention. It can be addicting, but the addiction is mostly based on a unique variety of topics and comfort felt by people who long for soul mates and a chance to share experiences and interests.

Another caveat: Just because you read something on an Internet website does not mean it is true. There is little review of the information on the Internet. Anyone can post information without fear of monitoring or critical analysis. Too many times our people take "literally" anything they read there and have to be encouraged to be skeptical of what the Internet offers.

Although the Internet is limited in its effectiveness, there is nothing limited about peer-support groups. They are very effective in many ways. It gives you a chance to understand that you are not alone. There is a sharing of experiences and discussions of ways to make our lives better. It is also very often fun. We on the spectrum are comfortable in these groups and enjoy each other. We meet and share experiences on a monthly basis or even more often. Mary and I met at such a group, although they are not generally great "pickup" spots for autistic people. Instead, they provide a great continual source of support for regular members. I know of at least a dozen such groups in my nation and frankly don't understand why more don't exist.

There is an entire chapter devoted to these groups in my first book, *Your Life is Not a Label: A Guide to Living Fully with Autism and Asperger's Syndrome*, also available from Future Horizons. The chapter covers the benefits of adult peer support groups and how to start them. I hope you take the time to read that chapter! In general, these groups run best when the autistic people have meetings at regular times and places with agendas. It is important to encourage all attendees to have at least one chance to be heard, for all new people to be introduced and for all personal discussions to remain confidential.

Talks at these meetings cover anything from issues at work to social concerns, school, finances and anything else pertinent. These groups usually work best when someone not on the spectrum helps facilitate them. Properly run, these groups eventually serve as circles in which all those who participate have an equal closeness to the person at the center.

The last growth option I will discuss is advocacy. That is also covered in greater detail in my other book. Advocacy is getting involved in programs that help others. It could be political, environmental, charitable, etc. The obvious advantages of advocacy are that we get to express our interest and work for something we believe in. Most causes are begging for people to stuff envelopes, proofread voter registration cards and do other necessary, incredibly repetitive campaign tasks that most people hate and many autistic people love to do!!

It is a positive experience to work on as many charities or projects as you can. The necessary factors these interactions bring of learning how to listen, cooperate and learn are constant benefits, above the good you may feel of helping others. That not only helps to get things done, but it also develops social skills that transfer to just socializing in the "friendship world." Advocacy definitely has a social side though. If you volunteer on any campaign that must be decided by an election, the campaign season usually involves different rallies and free events for volunteers, usually with an election night celebration, win or lose. For example, in 1992, my roommate and I practically moved into a campaign headquarters to volunteer and were rewarded with a free ride to a huge rally in Orange County, where we were just a few aisles away from the man who would become President of the United States.

The point of this is that advocacy not only expands your social abilities, but it actually includes new social opportunities with people who share a common goal. Many people have actually met and married, as a result of a campaign or other social activities I've mentioned several times in this book.

There is also the fact that many people have gotten jobs or found other opportunities because the person who could make that offer remembered them from a campaign or club. Activities like these and others we've mentioned can be enjoyed by all of us. Remember, we grow with each social experience we have.

In summary, there are avenues for us to grow and improve all through life. This should not end for us at a certain age or when artificial developmental deadlines are not met. We should continually try to expand our social contacts. It can be through clubs, support groups, advocacy centers, friends, the workplace, sporting events, dinners out with friends, the internet, plays, movies, etc.

If you are on the spectrum, like Mary and I, it is important that you never give up on the possibility of having a relationship. For me, it took 46 years of living. The important thing is that you should relax and enjoy your life while you wait for that relationship to come along. If you relax and enjoy the journey, it will!

If you are a parent, just enjoy the qualities that your son or daughter brings to you. Don't belabor the fact that they may not have a relationship. Focus on the many positives that they have brought, and will bring, to your life.

Life for those of us with autism or Asperger's, as life should be for everyone, must be a constant striving to make the most of every opportunity for growth available.

Is there hope for late bloomers? Indeed, there is!

Conclusion

Hopefully, this book has imparted enough information to open up the mysterious world of sex and social activity to you. We want you to be able to believe that this happiness is possible and therefore, take steps to achieve it! Sometimes this book says things the way they should be. Other times, it says things the way they simply are. Sometimes sexuality is brutally immoral, painful and politically or religiously incorrect. However, as we have said, it can be a wonderful, and fulfilling experience.

Please gain confidence and knowledge. Arm yourself well to go forth and conquer. Make your social/sex life the way you want it to be!

What has empowered me most in my life was to finally, after over forty-six years, to meet Mary, who loves me unconditionally. I have known many who loved me out of obligation and other noble reasons, but to be simply loved and accepted as I am, was a first. This is the most important gift that any of us can give to any other person, autistic or not.

Unconditional love should be the birthright of every human being and in the best of times, sexual experience can be the ultimate celebration of such a love shared by two adults.

If this book does nothing else, it must forever erase the lie that people with autism have little interest or potential to enjoy sexual curiosity, adventure and experience. In the sexual arena, as in others, we are just as human as the rest of you.

Jerry and Mary Newport

Tucson, Arizona

Glossary

Abortion: A surgical operation that terminates a pregnancy without birth taking place.

Abuse: Rape or sexual assault.

Adolescence: The period in which a young person grows into physical maturity, approximately between ages of thirteen and twenty.

AIDS/HIV: A retrovirus that causes severe deficiency in the immune system resulting in disease and often death.

Anal Intercourse: Intercourse in which the anus is penetrated.

Aspie: Term to describe someone with Asperger's Syndrome.

Autie: Popular descriptor for a person who is autistic.

Autism Spectrum: The entire range of possible combinations of attributes, challenges, symptoms and traits of autism, as well as frequency, intensity and duration that can be observed in an individual considered to have autism or Asperger's syndrome.

Breasts: Human Mammary Gland--A source of nourishment for newborn babies. Also an area that is usually highly sensitive while making out or during love making. One of the erogenous zones on a woman, or in some cases also a man.

Celibacy: A lifestyle that does not include sexual intercourse.

Child Support: Payments, usually resulting from a court order, to contribute to the support of a minor child.

Climax: The moment of orgasm, reached in sexual intercourse, or during masturbation. Climax is not always experienced by each partner at the same moment or even by both partners.

Conception: The creation of a baby in the Mother.

Condom: Thin sheath of latex or similar material, placed upon a penis prior to intercourse to reduce the possibility of pregnancy and to reduce the chances of disease.

Contraception: Any conscious effort or medication taken to prevent pregnancy.

Date Rape: Involuntary intercourse forced on the female by the male, during a date.

Diaphragm: Contraceptive device used by a female to prevent sperm from entering her uterus.

DNA: (Deoxyribonucleic Acid) Discovered by Nobel Laureates, Watson and Cruick. By examining the DNA of any person, his or her heritage can be ascertained. You can establish the identity of any person by examining any part of their body, skin or bodily fluid. Everyone's DNA is different.

Erogenous Zones: Pertaining to zones of the body sensitive to sexual stimulation. They include, but are not limited to; neck, ears, breasts, penis, vaginal area, inner thighs.

Fallopian Tubes: Two delicate tubes that connect the uterus to a pair of ovaries.

Fertilization: The union of sperm and ovum.

Foreplay: Heightened intimate activity intended to increase passion, interest and arousal prior to sexual intercourse.

Gay: A homosexual.

Gonorrhea: An STD (sexually transmitted disease) contracted during sexual intercourse. A common symptom is very uncomfortable burning during urination. Usually curable with shots of antibiotics.

Herpes: A disease that causes sores on the lips, mouth or genital area. Herpes simplex is what we commonly refer to as blisters or cold sores on the lips, and is not generally caused by sexual interaction. Herpes that erupt in the genital area are usually caused by sexual interaction with someone who has genital herpes. This disease is contagious at anytime, but particularly while the infected person has open sores. There are drugs to greatly reduce the effects of either Herpes, but no absolute cure is known at this time.

Homosexual: One who has sexual intercourse with people of the same gender.

Hormones: Internally secreted compounds that affect the function of specific organs or tissues. Hormones are transmitted by body fluids.

Hymen: Mucous membrane at opening of vagina, usually torn or broken during a woman's first sexual intercourse but may be accidentally torn or broken before that event.

Intercourse: Intense, intimate, physical connection of two sexual partners. In most cases this relates to the insertion of the male member (penis) into the female's vagina.

Labia: "Lips," lip-like folds that surround labia minor and vagina. Labia major surround Labia minor. Labia minor are smaller folds of skin, closer to vagina.

Lesbian: Female homosexual.

Lubricant: A jelly-like substance used to facilitate intercourse.

Masturbation: Manual act of self-inducing an orgasm by stimulation of appropriate pubic regions.

Molestation: Repeated violation of physical boundaries, resulting in injury and humiliation.

Monogamous: Having sexual intercourse with only one partner on a regular basis.

Necking: Kissing and hugging between two consenting people. Could lead to fondling of breasts and other erotic areas.

Neurotypical: Generally used to refer to people who are normal or typical of the majority of the population.

Oral Sex: Not to be confused with talking about sex or kissing. It is the act of placing one's mouth on the genitals of another person to cause excitement and possible climax.

Orgasm: In male, when the penis ejaculates semen. In female, a sudden final stiffening of pubic regions, accompanied by steadily increasing heartbeat, followed immediately by relaxation.

Ovaries: Glands that stimulate maturation of eggs.

Ovulation: Release of the most mature egg, halfway through the 28 day menstrual cycle.

Ovum: Female reproductive cell; gamete.

Penis: Male reproductive organ.

Petting: Stroking and touching of breast and other parts in preparation for sexual intercourse.

Pill: Popular term for a birth control pill, taken by female to avoid pregnancy, on a daily basis. "Morning after" pill is taken to avoid pregnancy if sexual intercourse occurred and the daily birth control pill was not taken on schedule.

Planned Parenthood: A non-profit organization with the mission of education and counseling to prevent unwanted pregnancy or sexually transmitted diseases.

Platonic Relationship: A friendship between two people who could be sexual partners but don't include this as part of the relationship.

Pregnant: Carrying a fertilized embryo that will become an infant.

Prophylactic: Cleansing, as in rendering free of sperm that can impregnate a woman.

Puberty: The age when a human body begins a biological change into the body of a sexually mature adult.

Rape: When a person is forced to have sexual intercourse or other sexual activity by a rapist. This is an illegal act punishable up to life imprisonment.

Rubber: Common usage to describe a condom, inspired by the rubber-like material.

Scrotum: Layer of skin that encases the testicles.

Semen: Fluid released in orgasm of the penis. Fertile semen contains enough sperm to impregnate a fertile female.

Sensual: Pertaining to experiences of senses during sexual activity. Sexually Transmitted Disease: An "STD" is a disease that is transmitted as a result of sexual activity.

Sperm: Male reproductive cells. Located in the male testicles. They travel during intercourse from the testicles, up through the penis and eject into the vagina of the female. Once there, they travel on their own to the uterus, where they unite with the female egg and can form a baby. Under the microscope, they resemble small tadpoles, and actually do a swimming motion when in the female vagina.

Spermicide: Placed in vagina, prior to intercourse, to kill entering sperm. It can be a gel, suppository, foam or film.

Sterilize: To make a woman incapable of becoming pregnant or a man incapable of making a woman pregnant.

Syphilis: An STD - a venereal disease that is characterized by local formation of sores, skin ulcers. If untreated by strong antibiotics can lead to paralysis. If it gets into the blood stream, has been known to be harmful to the entire system, including the brain and can even cause death.

Tubal Ligation: An operation in which the fallopian tubes of a female are cauterized by an electric spark. This closes them and prevents any ovum from exposure to sperm. This operation sterilizes the female.

Testicles: The male reproductive gland, source of sperm. Located in the scrotum.

Uterus: located in the pelvic area of the female. It receives and holds the fertilized egg during its growth process.

Vagina: The channel leading from the outside to the uterus.

Vaginal Foam: Also commonly referred to as spermicide. It is a foam that acts to destroy sperm in the vagina so it cannot travel to the uterus.

Vas Deferens: Tube that runs from the testicles.

Vasectomy: An operation in which the vas deferens is cut to eliminate the flow of sperm. This operation is reversible in some cases.

Venereal Disease: Any of several contagious diseases, such as syphilis or gonorrhea, contracted through sexual intercourse.

Virgin: A person who has not experienced sexual intercourse.

Withdrawal: The act of drawing back from a person, experience or event. In sexual terms, it is the act of removing the penis from the vagina.

Book List

Adolescents and Adults with Asperger's Syndrome (Inge Wakehurst Trust, 1992)

Asperger's and Adolescence, by Teresa Bolick (2001, Future Horizons, Inc.)

Asperger's and Self-Esteem, by Norm Ledgin (2002, Future Horizons, Inc)

Asperger's Syndrome and Adolescence - Practical Solutions for School Success by Brenda Smith Myles (2001, Autism Asperger's Publishing Company)

Asperger's Syndrome and Difficult Moments by Brenda Smith Myles, Ph.D., and Jack Southwick (2000, Future Horizons, Inc)

Asperger's Syndrome, A Guide for Parents and Professionals by Tony Attwood (1998, Jessica Kingsley)

Asperger's-What Does It Mean to Me? by Catherine Faherty (2000, Future Horizons, Inc)

Autism in Adolescents and Adults, by Eric Schopple and Gary B. Mesibov, Ed. (1983, Plenum Press)

Autism/Asperger's-Solving the Relationship Puzzle, by Steven E. Gutstein (2001, Future Horizons, Inc.)

Inclusive Programming for Middle School Students with Autism/Asperger's Syndrome, by Sheila Wagner (2001, Future Horizons, Inc.)

Navigating the Social World, by Jeanette McAfee, MD (2002, Future Horizons, Inc.)

The Oasis Guide, by Patricia Romanowski Bashe and Barbara L. Kirby (2001, Crown Publishers)

Sex Education: Issues for The Person with Autism, by Nancy J. Dalrymple and Barbara Porco (1991, Indiana Resource Center for Autism)

Sexuality and People with Intellectual Disability, by Ben Feingold (1997, Paul H. Brooks)

Taking Care of Myself, by Mary Wroble (2003, Future Horizons, Inc.)

Your Life is Not a Label, by Jerry Newport (2001, Future Horizons, Inc.)

Addendum

Jerry Newport and Mary Insight—As interviewed by Veronica Palmer for the Autism/Asperger's Digest Magazine on Social Relationships

One Size Does Not Fit All

A/AD: *Mary and Jerry, thanks for inviting Future Horizons to help you compose this chapter on relationships. Because it's such a broad topic, in this chapter we'd like to concentrate on social relationships as you were growing up, talking just briefly about college and work. Then let's get down to the interesting and personal questions about romantic relationships, that I'm sure all our readers are interested in.*

Jerry: No problem. A lot of people have fantasies about what it is like for two people with the same challenge to marry, and we'd be doing our readers a disservice if we didn't talk about it.

Mary: Jerry isn't saying that it doesn't work, but that it takes a lot more daily work than either of us new the first time around.

Jerry: We're a lot smarter now, (laughter) but we'll get back to that later.

A/AD: *To start, why did you choose the title, "One Size Does Not Fit All"?*

Jerry: Because males and females with AS, autism or any disability, don't develop socially in the same way.

A/AD: *How do you think the sex difference plays out?*

Mary: Society expects different things of men and women, socially. One sex is supposed to be the hunter and the other is the caretaker, the nurturer. That means that some traits will be more noticeable in boys than in girls: for instance, shyness in boys and aggressive behaviors in girls.

Jerry: A boy who doesn't make eye contact is going to be noticed more than a girl that doesn't have it. A boy who fusses about getting over-stimulated will stand out more than a girl who does the same thing. Certain Asperger's behaviors tend to fit a female stereotype more than they fit a male stereotype. That's probably why a lot of women who have the condition aren't being diagnosed. There's an interesting study about this by two Swedish researchers, Svenny Koop and Christophe Gilberg [European Child and Adolescent Psychiatry – 1992] They feel that if you remove gender bias, the male/female ratio for AS is much closer – maybe three to two, if not one to one. I bet that is also true across the autism spectrum.

A/AD: So you're saying that society reinforces more overt, group activities for boys, while reinforcing more docile, quiet and one-to-one behavior for girls?

Jerry: Passive behavior is much more acceptable for girls. Men are supposed to initiate socially. That's something you rarely find in AS. They usually show more initiative than high-functioning folks or regular autistic people. But in comparison to the rest of society, we are not really initiators. A passive woman will attract a lot of men. Too often, she attracts the wrong kind, domineering and abusive. That is not a scientific statement. It is based on what a lot of women have shared with me. However, a passive guy will not attract a lot of women.

Mary: When I sought a diagnosis, I was told that first, autism was not likely because I am female. The historically observed male to female ratio does affect the diagnosis process.

A/AD: *Do you think the gender differences play out in terms of any of the sensory problems or the types of repetitive stereotypic interests?*

Jerry: Sensory issues prevent most AS men from enjoying things like team sports, especially. That is an important bonding activity. You don't have to be any good at it but it's a group thing. You earn respect from peers just for taking part in the action. On the other hand, little girls aren't necessarily expected to enjoy those things. They have a lot less pressure to be in group activities. They have stuff like dollhouses to stim on.

Mary: I'm no statistics expert, but I do know that guys get busted for sensory sensitivity more than females because of gender bias. One thing that is overlooked on the sensory issue for females is anemia. Before my hysterectomy, I was crippled from photosensitivity and seizures. When my iron level rose to normal, those problems went into 100 percent remission.

A/AD: *How early do you remember trying to have any kind of social contact with another person?*

Jerry: My first clear memory was at Thanksgiving in 1952. I was four. We went to Uncle Bob's house and there were younger relatives present. I could see that in this large group the younger people entered the group interaction with ease that I lacked. That was my first experience with feeling out of sync and not liking it. Another experience came about a year and a half later. I walked home with a couple of people from kindergarten. It was a small town in upstate New York and we didn't have to worry about our safety. We came to a vacant lot and they played keep-away. When they threw the ball in my direction and I caught it, they rushed me like they knew I wouldn't know what to do. I walked home, looked in the mirror and asked myself, "What did they see? I look like my brothers; I look like everybody else. What is it about me that people see?" I was between five and six.

Mary: It was easier to form friendships up to the fourth grade. My early friends tell me, to this day, that they enjoyed my unusual play and were bored when my family moved away. My early friends enjoyed spinning with me. They enjoyed my unihibited weirdness. Autistic doesn't have to mean friendless.

A/AD: *So, at a very young age you were aware of being different?*

Jerry: I was aware of the difference but I didn't have a name for it. But it was such a subtle difference that I wasn't obsessed with it.

Mary: I became aware of my difference in the fourth grade. My earlier friends imitated me, but at a new school with new kids, they hated me for being so different.

A/AD: *Did you feel a need to "fit in" or to be like other people?*

Jerry: I don't know about wanting to be like other people. I just wanted to have friends. I was always kind of outspoken and actually I prided myself on being somewhat outspoken. I read history books at an early age and I knew that stuff like the revolution happened because some people said what nobody else was willing to. But I didn't want to be that way so much that I would be an outcast. As a kid, I felt like I was always five or ten minutes away from the next social blunder, where I would do or say something hopelessly awkward and everybody around me laugh. There was always that undercurrent.   But I never felt like an outcast.

Mary: Not until the seventh grade. Between the fourth and fifth grade, I was just me.   Starting with seventh grade, I tried really hard to fit in, using clothes, makeup and hairstyles. No matter how trendy and pretty I made myself, I still didn't fit in because my interests were so different.

A/AD: What helped you get ready to form your first friendships?

Jerry: Having to SHARE my parents with two old brothers was the main thing. I see too many families where the needs of the autistic person run the day.   There has to be balance, between that very needy person and needs of parents and siblings. I don't care how needy he is, he has to learn that he is not the sun with the rest of the world as planets revolving around his every tantrum. I was very lucky to have two older brothers and two parents whose egos weren't totally tied up in what I thought of them or how I succeeded.

The real key in social learning is that you have to share time, attention, activity. Without sharing, there is no friendship or relationships.

Here's an example.   One of our youngsters invited a classmate home. Then, he sat in front of his computer, doing all of the playing. The other kid just watched. The autistic kid was halfway there. He invited someone to come home and play. That is a huge step. But he still had an incomplete concept of friendship. His "friend" was a human piece of furniture to be around while he played just as he wanted, with his games and his rules.

The autistic kid thinks, "This is great, I have somebody here while I'm on my computer!" The other kid is bored.

Maybe you need to role play. Ask your autistic son if he would like to go to a restaurant and have to stand outside, look through the window and watch everyone eat.

Sharing is so hard because you have to give up control. You can't control what the other person will say or do. It was hard for me to allow even a hug because I had to trust that the other person, often bigger, wouldn't squeeze me too hard! The resistance to early sharing is very neurologically based.

So sharing involves giving up control and trust of someone else. That is an important bridge and the earlier it is crossed, the better! But to that, you have to help the child settle down and ABA and other intensive therapy only works on the brain and not the body. You have to develop both. I would say start with the body, first. School is dumb enough today that the brain has plenty of time.

When I had some years of exercise, sports, swimming, tumbling, etc. behind me, I relaxed. I didn't feel that I had to control the world around me. Finally, in fifth grade, I could walk into a school cafeteria, tune out enough noise and talk to other students. That is why small group activities are so important. You have to share the ball. You learn to be part of a group that works for a common goal. You can't be in chorus and sing what you want when you want. The same is true in band. But you sure feel good in a concert when it sounds right, after all.

I can't see how our kids will develop friendships until they learn to share like that. You don't learn that if everything is on a one-to-one basis with some help. One way or another, our children need inclusion in small, fun group activities.

Mary: Nothing prepared me for my first friendships. I was just wild and crazy and the young kids loved it. I was just me.

A/AD: *So you had active friendships when you were young? Or how did those go?*

Jerry: They were shallow friendships, most of them formed from Boy Scouts, swimming class or Little League. I didn't make friends just because they were people I knew at school. Some were classmates, but the connection surfaced from shared interests, rather than being in school together.

I don't remember opening up to anybody. I was always guarded in my conversation. I can't say that I had close friendships or relationships with anybody, even though there were a couple of people with whom I spent a lot of time. I think in comparison to the friendships that my schoolmates had, mine weren't nearly as deep. But in comparison to most people with Asperger's, I had more friends. I guess my last high school friend, Steve Lazzaro, was the only one who I ever halfway opened up to.

Mary: It was easier to have friendships at a younger age because younger children are less inhibited. As they mature, they try to be more sophisticated. They want social sameness. I think it's easier for an autistic to have earlier friendships because the nature of play is less sophisticated. That is the very reason pets such as dogs are so good. They just want to romp and play and love unconditionally.

A/AD: Did you choose to participate in these activities yourself, or did your parents prod you to be more involved socially?

Jerry: I had the good fortune of having two older brothers whose behavior I could model. My brothers were in Cub Scouts, I went to Cub Scouts. My older brother was in Little League, I went to Little League. My brothers played musical instruments so I played an instrument, too. Literally, everything I did through elementary school was simply copying what John and Jim did before me. That made it a lot easier.

Mary: My parents were totally aloof to my social life. We lived in a neighborhood with a number of children who were my age. We approached each other out of curiosity. I was always outside playing, doing things like spinning, rolling, tumbling on the front lawn or climbing trees. I was totally unsupervised (which I don't recommend), but it gave me exposure to other children.

A/AD: While you were in elementary school, do you remember anything special about getting along with your peers or your teachers?

Jerry: I got along better with teachers than peers. Sometimes I said or did things that squarely showed a lack of empathy toward my peers. I think what finally got me included in elementary school was people making a big fuss about me being a math brain. They showed me off to new students. It was a unique identity.

My father helped me share my skill by teaching me all of the sports numbers. Soon I was the one who kept everybody informed on all of the sports statistics and stuff. But the lack of empathy was a barrier.

Mary: I, too, got along with teachers better than children. Teachers liked my early talents in music and art. They tried to help me become more socially acceptable.

After the sixth grade, I no longer had one teacher all day. I had seven! That was a disaster because I became a face in the crowd and the one-on-one relationships disappeared. I went from an A student to a D student with one friend who did everything to corrupt me.

A/AD: How involved were you in sports?

Mary: I loved kickball and played as well as the boys, so I played with the boys a lot. They couldn't allow themselves to like me openly. Social stigma. But they always wanted me on their teams.

Jerry: I loved to play them but I wasn't very good. My favorite sport was baseball. I became a decent hitter but my fielding stank. I loved to ride my bicycle. It was fun in the fall when hurricanes came. I sailed home on them, letting the wind fill up an empty paper-route bag.

A couple of guys tried to teach me to play tennis but that was hopeless. Even though I wasn't very good at sports, I'm glad that I was given a chance to fail. I ran track and cross country for four years and never won a race. But it got me in good shape and helped me focus. My grades improved every year that I ran.

A/AD: What did the failure teach you?

Jerry: That it was okay to fail—a very important lesson to learn. You need to be able to fail.

Mary: In my family, failure was a cause for ostracization. Any failure devastated me.

A/AD: How did you relate to your math abilities? Did it contribute to your sense of self-esteem?

Jerry: I think people who have special skills, real savant-level skills like Mary's and mine, are misunderstood.

I remember in third grade somebody was showing me off to somebody else. I multiplied some numbers for them and I saw, out of the corner of my eye, that somebody was looking at me and doing some nonverbal signal to indicate that while I was very good in this one area I was really kind of "off" otherwise.

From that day on, my attitude towards numbers and math in general was, "If I don't have to work at it, it's okay." But I wasn't really interested in it. I go into this in detail in another chapter so that's it for now.

A/AD: Getting back to that gender difference, did the girls accept you more than the boys did?

Jerry: In elementary school, I had little contact with girls, other than if a girl sat next to me in a class, we'd occasionally say, 'Hello.' My contact was exclusively with either teachers or the boys. I noticed the pretty ones but was too in awe of them to do more than look.

A/AD: Mary, did you find that girls accepted you more easily than did boys?

Mary: Boys accepted me more than girls. I shared their interests and was very rough and tumble.

A/AD: *Did you have to be taught some of the social skills that neurotypical kids have? Did your parents spend time with you practicing?*

Jerry: My parents saw that I was a wallflower but they weren't comfortable discussing it with me. The best attempt they made was hinting that I should ask out the daughter of some people they played bridge with. Her steady dates were guys who could have crushed me like a beer can! They hoped that maybe my middle brother would teach me but he was in college too soon to do that. They probably regarded themselves as late bloomers too and weren't too worried about me. I remember them talking about how other students came back from a couple of years of college, "all grown up."

When I was a senior in high school, my friend Steve, said, "Jerry, you have to make a conscious effort to do what the rest of us do naturally."

And he was absolutely right. I still know that guy; he's in Manhattan. He was very opposite of me in many ways. He was always well groomed and socially appropriate. But we had great memories in common. I had to deliberately think about how to behave and how to react in certain situations where other people could just do those things without thinking.

The first really embarrassing moment for me was in sixth grade. We were in a structured dance class, ballroom dancing. It was easy to pick up the dance patterns. That was kind of fun. By then, I could tolerate holding a girl's hand and putting my arm around her waist. So the night arrived when it was time to show us off to our parents.

Everyone is crowded into our combination auditorium/ gymnasium, and we're dancing. The next dance was a ladies' choice. However, I didn't realize that. So the ladies are on one side and the boys on the other. I went over to the girl's side trying to pick my next partner. They're all looking at me really confused. Suddenly the whole place was just a sea of laughter, and I realized what I had done.

It took me a good two years to work up the courage to ask anybody to dance after that, because I was just so humiliated. The dance that broke the streak was Chubby Checker's "Twist." If you have any autism at all, you have to twist!

Mary: My parents themselves lacked any social skills. They taught me nothing. My neighbors (in the 6th-9th grades) taught me etiquette and grooming. They didn't let me be an autistic slob. They helped me learn manners and beauty. To this day, I thank them.

A/AD: Did these embarrassing moments happen a lot in school?

Jerry: Well, not a lot, but the problem I had (which I share with my peers) was that my recovery time was very long. Most kids, if they had done something like that, would laugh it off. Maybe they'd feel funny for a couple of days, but that would be it. It wouldn't take them two years to recover.

The problem I had then, and the problem I see today in my adult peers, is that they don't engage in social experiences often enough to wade through the learning curve. It takes them so long to recover from one disappointment and then try again that there is no learning curve.

A/AD: Why do you think the recovery process is so long?

Jerry: We try so hard to find sanity in our world. When we screw up like that publicly, it hurts more than it would for a kid who's not spending most of his time waging war with the world.

That's the thing. I was spending a lot of time just at war with the world rather than feeling a peaceful existence within it in comparison to normal kids.

Mary: The recovery process is so long because of the ridicule factor. No one praised me for my skills. I just got ridiculed.

A/AD: Did you feel angry towards the kids? Did it make you feel depressed?

Mary: I wasn't so angry as depressed. That's not to say I wasn't angry. It is just that the depression was overwhelming. I wanted to die.

Jerry: I don't remember feeling angry at that age; maybe envious at times. From the minute I saw that kid sending out that signal to the other kids, "Well, I don't care how fast he can multiply, he's still a nut.", I've got to say for the next 35 to 40 years I spent most of my time wanting to be anybody but me. I looked at my math talent as a curse rather than a blessing. I remember thinking, "I guess I have to live with this and make the most of it, but it doesn't mean I like it."

I wanted to be anybody but Jerry Newport. I was angrier with me than with the people around me.

A/AD: Mary, was your experience the same, or is it different for girls?

Mary: By the seventh grade, I was keenly aware that I was a nerd. Embarrassment happened daily when I was ridiculed. I just came apart and couldn't function. This is where etiquette, beauty and becoming sexy helped out. It helped me dig myself out of the nerddom and enter a social circle.

Did I say, "sexy?" Yes. Face it.

Sexual interest begins in the seventh and eighth grades because of puberty. Becoming sexy and beautiful can especially help a girl find social interest. Face it. You need to have that sex talk. Sudden beauty attracts sudden interest and girls, especially, need sex education.

A/AD: Was jealousy part of your peer experience?

Jerry: I felt very misunderstood because most of my peers were jealous of me for having this skill – jealous to the point that times when I was about to make a fool of myself again, they rejoiced. I felt jealous of them. They were part of the flock in a way that I didn't feel like I was.

Mary: If it was jealousy, it was expressed as pure hatred.

A/AD: Did you keep all of this to yourself or were there people you talked to about it?

Jerry: I never talked to anybody about it – not my brothers or even my parents. I just kept it all in.

A/AD: How about you, Mary?

Mary: No one talked with me. I kept it all to myself.

A/AD: Jerry, did you keep all of these feelings to yourself because you didn't want to talk about them, or because you didn't know how to put them into words?

Jerry: That's the way my family handled things. I can remember in my house whenever my parents reached a point in any discussion where there was emotional content, it felt like the whole place was about ready to crash. Neither one of my parents wanted to deal with anything like that openly.

Mary: Ditto.

A/AD: *Tell us a little bit more about your family relationships.*

Jerry: I was always afraid of my dad because he was so big. Yet he was not an abusive guy at all.

My oldest brother was seven years ahead of me and it seemed like by the time I was old enough to have even a halfway intelligent conversation with him, he was off to college. So it was Jim that I knew better. Jim was a little less than three years older than me. He was, by far, the more advanced person socially of any of us. Some of my friends would see Jim, who was dating girls even in sixth and seventh grade, and say, 'Well, why is your brother so cool and you're not?'

The three of us were not close; we tolerated each other. My older brothers are like oil and water. They were rivals for parental attention. I was like a neutral little country in comparison. I never got any attention in the way I wanted. I got way too much of the attention that I didn't want. Nobody ever told me I was popular, coordinated or cool. They always told me how smart I was until I was sick of hearing it.

Back to my older brothers. It seemed as if we had an unspoken treaty where we agreed not to kill each other because we would all eventually grow up and escape. It seemed like all of us felt like prisoners in that family.

My mom and dad got married for whatever reason, but by the time the three of us were born, they were sleeping in separate beds. I remember watching my dad in his car. He was always happy when he drove away and scared when he came back. It seemed that if there was any activity to do to keep away from home, he did it. A lot of fathers do that in our community.

They were very responsible, and totally involved in the community, volunteering. After my older brother got married, at one point he asked my parents to talk to his therapist. They refused. My dad had a classic response, "Your mother and I have co-existed peacefully for almost forty years and you have to learn to do the same." There is a huge difference between that and marriage. I mean, can you imagine Khrushchev married to Kennedy?

Mary: I was ostracized by everyone in my family. It was pure hell to have almost everyone hate me. My parents did nothing to mediate family relationships. There was a lot of sibling violence among seven children. And my only friend was violent toward me. All of this made me take a vow in the fifth grade that none of this would ever happen if I had a family. I lived up to it.

A/AD: *It must have been a difficult environment for your social and emotional development.*

Mary: It wasn't just difficult. It was devastating. My daily schedule was to go to school, get ridiculed, and beat up. After school, to my "friend's" house and get beat up. Dinnertime, go home, get ridiculed and beat up. I was suicidal.

Jerry: Mom and Dad stayed married for us boys. It had to be very unsatisfying for both. It does a lot to explain Dad's smoking and their obesity. Trying to work with me on social stuff would have opened up all of the wounds.

A/AD: Puberty is a highly emotional time for most kids. How did that affect your relationships?

Jerry: Once I discovered my natural erector set, I became obsessed with it and that really bothered my parents. They finally took me to see the school psychologist to see if he could straighten me out on that point. [laughter] The problem was that I was too straight!!

This was when I started thinking about dating. Some of my friends dated already. By the end of the eighth grade at least half a dozen of my classmates were regularly dating. And by the end of ninth grade, a whole lot more were dating. In tenth grade there were still enough other people not dating that we could show up at a party solo and that would be OK.

At the beginning of my sophomore year somebody threw a party and my best friend told me that I couldn't go because they knew I wouldn't have a date. Looking back, I wish I had said to him, 'How did you get your date?' That might have led in some positive direction. But I just saw a wall.

It was two more years before I had a date. The frustration I experienced is probably what most kids today are experiencing in sixth, seventh, and eighth grade. It's happening earlier. Middle school today is just the absolute pits. I didn't get picked on because my parents were teachers and it was a small high school, but I was lucky.

Mary: Puberty helped in some respects because I became sexy. I did everything to cultivate my looks. My peer's reactions began to change in the ninth grade. I was not ridiculed so much. Puberty was hard because adults were having sex with me and offering me marijuana, alcohol and LSD.

I totally came apart at the seams and became incommunicado. My parents put me in a cult. Out of sight, out of mind.

A/AD: What advice would you give someone with AS in seventh or eighth grade about helping himself socially?

Jerry: I would tell him to be realistic and say, "Look around your class. I'll bet you'll find some girls out there who feel just as left out as you do."

Heck, most of them have this self-destructive fantasy that dating some normal girl will be the best thing for their image. Heck, why not date a young girl with some other kind of challenge, not necessarily autism? There might be more empathy to share.

What kids really need at that age is practice. They need to acquire comfort and experience in simple, shared experiences. That's the first step. Instead of fixating on some class queen, be realistic and you'll have much better success.

I'd also suggest they seek out girls or guys who have common interests. It could be they like to read the same kind of books, or have the same favorite subjects you have. Common interests are a good way to start building relationships.. Also, do things on weekends with other people who don't have dates, either. Isolation just leads to social stagnancy.

Mary: Do everything to look and act like everyone else. That's the rule in adult life, too.

A/AD: Do you think part of the social developmental process for you was just getting a little bit older? Did things ease up as you got into high school and you just understood things more?

Jerry: Socializing got easier the last couple of years of high school. When I got a driver's license, I was somebody that could give other people rides to places. [laughter] I finally worked up the courage to go out a few times, my senior year.

Mary: My social life improved in high school as far as peers go. It was the adults in my life who made me crack.

A/AD: What other strategies worked for you in social situations as a teenager?

Mary: I only had relationships with adults. None of my friends were my age. My parents got rid of me because of this. I got no help.

Jerry: Well, I don't know. I went out with girls a few years younger than I was and from neighboring towns. I figured they didn't know I was a hopeless nerd or they didn't know enough to reject me.

You know, when you're a senior and they're a freshman, they are so impressed by the fact that you're a senior, you don't have to work hard at the rest of it. I didn't have good social coping skills. I just had the advantage of age. [laughter]

A/AD: It sounds like you had a healthy dose of self-esteem. So many kids with AS don't have any.

Jerry: I had more than the average peer, but my self-esteem was really skewed. If you charted my self-esteem there would be a high point if you asked me, "Well, how do you feel about your professional potential? Do you think you will grow up, go to college, graduate and make a lot of money?"

But if you asked me questions like, "Do you think people really like you? Do you think you'll ever be somebody that people really want to be around or will they just tolerate you because you're so smart?" then you would have seen real doubt.

Even though I wasn't crazy about math, it was there. Whether or not I wanted to spend a lot of time on it, it was part of my act. I think my self-esteem in general was maybe higher than most of my Asperger's peers. The big difference was that I would take a social risk. But in comparison to society in general, my self-esteem was lower. It was in college that I became more aware of that. However high my self-esteem was in comparison to peers, it still caused problems.

A/AD: Jerry, how did your lack of self-esteem, compared to most people, cause problems?

Jerry: The main problem was my lack of social discretion. I did dangerous things to win social approval. It started in high school.

At a couple of parties, the other guys wanted to see how much I could drink, so I obliged. The first time, I was only fourteen, and when I got sick to the vomiting stage, they called my father to pick me up.

The other time, I was a senior and got really smashed. They let me drive home. It was a win-win situation for them.

They got to see me "drive funny" and if I had crashed on the way home, they could have said, "Look at what crazy Newport did!"

It got worse in college. As a senior turning twenty-one, tradition was that you went down to a local bar and had twenty-one beers. I had a phony ID and went along. I decided to drink twenty-one myself, just to show I could do it. I managed to do it but was quite out of it.

Fortunately, I did not drive that night. Later, I began smoking pot and using drugs to fit in with the bell-bottom crowd.

The irony was that others took these drugs to feel messed up. They made me feel normal! The common denominator in a room full of high people is like group autism. Nobody really communicates. People stare off into space, perseverate on ice cream and pizza crusts and say, "Groovy" or "Far out."

I fit in more in that social arena, actually an antisocial arena, than normal. My great visual memory enabled me to replay these "trips" so I actually didn't use drugs as often as some others. But street drugs are dangerous because you have no guarantee of what you have consumed.

To sum it up, the real danger of relatively low self-esteem is that a person can be so desperate to make friends that he shows poor judgment. He does dangerous things to win social approval. I was very lucky to survive the drinking and drugs.

A/AD: Mary, how about you? What was your self-esteem like?

Mary: I had no self-esteem.

A/AD: Mary, you became a parent at a young age. How did your AS influence your relationship with the fathers of your children, and your children themselves?

Mary: I got married at age sixteen. It was an arranged marriage. That was a cult practice. My marriage was terrible because there was no love, just sex. When I became pregnant, it was a joyous occasion. I was bringing someone into the world who would love me. I knew my baby wouldn't despise me for being different like my husband did.

There was a lot of love between my sons and me. I did everything to protect them from bad school situations. I home schooled them in their middle school years. If there were problems, we talked about them. AS was a strong point in raising my children because of my savant talents. I helped my children with their gifts.

Jerry: If I can interject something here... Mary did a remarkable job as a mom, with little support. Her sons were better off being home-schooled overall. They are grown, responsible adults now. They are much better adjusted than we were at their ages.

A/AD: Jerry, did you find it easier or more difficult to make friends once you went off to college?

Jerry: I found it easier. One of the reasons I went to Michigan was to be anonymous. I was seven hundred miles away from my hometown, and out of 35,000 people, only one senior knew who I was. I moved into the dormitory and fell in with the rest of the dorm. We did lots of things together.

Freshmen there were at a real disadvantage socially because there were almost three men to every woman on the undergraduate level. So, to not have a date on a weekend was not a big deal. Most of my freshmen peers didn't. During my first year there were a couple incidents where people tried to send me signals.

I went out with a girl from my math class and I thought we had a good time, so I asked her out about 13 or 14 times. I asked her out so many times that she quit the math class to get away from me. A guy in my dorm came up to me one day and said, "Jerry can we talk? You know this girl named Becky? You realize you've asked her out 14 times? Don't you get it? She's not interested in you."

After that, I went by the three-strike rule. I felt badly that apparently she dropped out of a class to avoid me. It was pretty humiliating to feel I'd done that to somebody.

Other people commented on strange things I did to get attention.

Occasionally in high school I tried to be the class clown, which didn't work. The teachers told my parents, who were teachers, and that ended it. In college I tried to do things to gain attention and impress my friends that were inappropriate. My dorm mates let me know about it. I joined a fraternity right away, because I thought frats were cool and I wanted to be cool. It was that simple [laughter]. I must have rushed a dozen houses and one asked me to be a member and I pledged. I would have pledged any house that asked me. I just wanted to be in a fraternity.

Mary: I was twenty-three and a single mother when I went to college. It was music school. It was easier to make friends because we were all a little kooky. There was mutual respect for our gifts. I liked college because people were mature and it was much easier to find a social circle.

A/AD: What about dating during these years?

Jerry: I developed some practical ways for me to find dates in college. I looked for girls who did something that interested me. Maybe they had read a book that I had read, or maybe a common book we had for a subject. The school was so big that it wasn't surprising at all to see somebody else carrying the same textbook you were carrying. Or I would notice that they were members of a certain sorority – I'm a Greek, she's a Greek. It was a connection, some excuse to talk to them.

And the funny thing I remember is that it really didn't matter who the girl was or whether we had anything in common or not. I would go out with anybody who would keep going out with me. Until they decided not to go out with...they always had the upper hand. Each girl was THE one, until she decided she wasn't the one.

It was funny, because I wound up with some very, very attractive freshmen. I remember one girl in particular, somebody I met during orientation. She grew up in Ann Arbor, so she already knew the college, very intimately.

She immediately pledged the most popular sorority on campus and she was not only very attractive, but a very mature, well-dressed girl, just an absolute doll. Here I am an absolute turkey taking her to my pledge formal. The guys in my house were quite mystified about how I managed to do that. I guess that at first, a lot of girls would find my genuine curiosity about them to be attractive. Being a math major was no longer seen as something to shy away from, and they're sitting there thinking, "I probably wouldn't have anything to do with this guy in high school, but five to ten years from now he might be a good bet." [laughter].

College students are more open socially.   But, I remember a story that fits in here.

It was the middle of my sophomore year.   I lived in a fraternity house. One day, I heard a bunch of my fellow sophomores sitting in a room discussing me. I walked right by the room and they just kept on talking. I guess they figured I was so out of it that I didn't hear them. And they were saying things like, "Yeah he can get a date with anybody." And somebody else would say, "Yes, once." Then somebody said, "You don't suppose old Newport is one of those idiot savants, do you?"

This was 1968.   I went to the library and looked up the term *savant* and I found a picture of this guy in an institution in France who could multiply and do calendar dates.   I thought, "Well, there's just not enough here to relate to.   I've never been in an institution, and I'm never going to be. I can't possibly be like one of these people."

That was my first exposure to anything ever remotely connected with autism. It was almost 20 years later that I had any further exposure to it.

Mary: Dating was much easier because music was a common interest. I also dated non-musicians. My identity was musician-artist. I did everything to be attractive and it worked, socially.

A/AD: *What dating tips would you pass along if someone is going to college?*

Jerry: Tips...well, as if I'm an expert.   I'd say number one is to accept who you are. My biggest problem was always trying to be someone else. When I went out with girls I either said nothing or talked all night in an effort to try to impress them. Neither approach worked. They don't want to do all the talking and they don't want to do all the listening. I never found a middle gear.

First, be yourself. If you are really yourself and comfortable with yourself, than you should be comfortable sharing the conversation.

Second, be realistic. Go out with women you've got something in common with, that you can share.

Third, be patient. A big problem with me was I had this fantasy that all my friends went to bed with girls on their first or second date. It didn't work that way. I knew guys who had girlfriends from their freshman year. They were seniors and pinned,* and they were still virgins.

Just be patient, for God's sake. On the first three or four dates you shouldn't be worrying about whether to kiss them or anything else. The main thing is, "Are you comfortable around this person or are you constantly feeling like you're stepping on eggs and you're doing or saying something that upsets them?"

Sometimes you might end up as friends, but romance is not meant to be. When things are working, it's effortless. In a certain sense, a hand fits a glove. But you still have to work at it.

Another rule, a good one: three strikes. If you ask someone out three times and it's always "no," forget it. There's three billion other fish out there. Too many of my peers get really stuck on one person, usually for the wrong reason, and just keep trying and failing.

received a fraternity pin.

Oh, one more. If you don't have a date and it's a weekend, go out anyway. Find some dateless gender peers and share an activity. See a movie or a game. Go to a poetry reading. Show some independence and you'll feel a lot better than being alone. You will also learn some things, and it is amazing how many single people you will see, of the opposite gender, doing this to. It makes you look more attractive, not less.

But the main thing—and parents reading this, listen up—is that the earlier in life that you start, the better.

Mary: Do everything to be like others. That's the rule at work, too. "But I'm autistic" doesn't cut it. Finding a person's interest helps. It's good conversation and it helps you grow. People are flattered if you want to hear about their interests. Jerry and I both used autism to help us make sense of our lives and negotiate with a non-autistic world.

Too many of our peers see a new diagnosis as an excuse to go off at anyone, any time. That's social suicide. If it wasn't for Jerry's involvement in the autism community , the word would never come up. Autism just isn't a big deal now.

A/AD: *Was sex on your mind a lot when you were in college?*

Jerry: Oh, all the time. ALLLL the time. I was on a crusade to find a perfect girl to convince everybody who had ever known me that I really wasn't a crazy person after all. I'd think, "Look at this beautiful girl. If she loves me, then you should, too."

It was a much, much bigger deal than it should have been. And that girl would have been a pretty piece of furniture to make me look good.

Mary: Sex was of great interest. I had several lovers. I was devastated that none of them wanted to get married. I was looking for a husband. They were looking for casual relationships.

A/AD: *Was sex part of your college experience?*

Jerry: Well, my left hand was sure interested in it. I tell you, if I'd put lipstick on my left hand I probably would have gotten engaged to it. I think I had an unusual amount of interest in it and frustration with not actually experiencing it. My first experience was pretty hilarious. It was about the end of my sophomore year when I visited San Francisco with a hooker. I was probably the most passive trick she'd ever had in her career. But it's funny. If I mention that I had any sex in college, it impresses most AS male peers.

Mary: Yes.

A/AD: *One of the things I've read is that some men with AS feel they have to have a woman. It becomes almost an obsession.*

Jerry: Boy, you've got that right. I spent more time in the last two and a half years of college trying to line up my next date than I spent studying. I wasted so much time. Several girlfriends lasted anywhere from three to six months, but the reason none of those relationships ever went anywhere was because I didn't have any sense of direction about my future, and I didn't have any real self-confidence. So, once people started to get to know me they could see that my interest in them was really superficial.

Mary: Men with AS have it harder than women, socially. Women can just get hair and wardrobe to be sexy. Women aren't held to macho standards like men. We're just kooky girls with great hair, wardrobes and bodies.

A/AD: Where do you think it comes from?

Jerry: It comes from the frustration of our youth. Most of the people I know who have really gone overboard in that direction are twenty-five or older and never had a date.

A/AD: Is it a longing to connect with another person?

Jerry: Absolutely. It's a total fantasy. They want this thing so badly, yet they're clueless about getting anywhere close to it. The saddest thing is that the older they are, the harder it is for them to ever get in that ballpark.

Check this out: The number one reason that my male peers lose jobs and have legal trouble is from inappropriate behavior, often seen as "stalking." They don't know what they are doing, at work or other places.

In elementary school, most of my friends experienced a gradual escalation of contact with girls. For me, I was just oblivious to them. I did miss out on some of that contact, but in comparison with most of my peers, I didn't miss out on nearly as much. It wasn't like I had the automatic stigma of being in special class or walking around with an adult albatross, an "aide," attached to me. Aides are a mixed blessing and the sooner your child can shed them, the better. Socially, they are the kiss of death.

I see too many parents harp on the academic side. That's because it's simple and predictable, compared to social growth.

Let's face it: you only need a two-word vocabulary to get a college degree now: "Point" and "Click." This is a generation that uses little calculators to do arithmetic. Critical thinking has all but disappeared from the curriculum. Give me a break.

Our kids don't become miserable adults because of brain shortages. It's the social stuff. The longer they wait to start learning social skills, the harder it is. The older they get, the more it means to them, and the more anxious they are. If they even get half a chance to do something, they are so full of self-consciousness and anxiety they almost invariably drive the other person away. You have to start them young. Let them kick and scream all they want. Better earlier than later.

Most women don't find my peers attractive socially because they lack confidence. They're so self-conscious. Nobody wants to spend an evening with somebody who's constantly fumbling, stuttering, tripping and insecure.

Men are supposed to be the captain of the ship, right? It's not fun for a girl to be out on this boat for the evening, constantly picking the captain up off the deck, reminding him where the ship's supposed to go, reassuring him that it's not sinking.

Women don't want to be put in that position. They want at least some illusion that the guy knows what he's doing. Even though most men don't know what they're doing anyway! I don't have to tell you that. [laughter]

A/AD: *That's right; it has nothing to do with Asperger's.* *[laughter]*

Jerry: But most men at least know how to fake it. We don't

know how to fake it because with guys with AS, what you see is what you get. By the same token, my brothers and my father expected me to be a good card player like them, especially with my memory. But I wasn't because I couldn't run a bluff. I was too busy, arranging all of the cards by number and suit. I remember one day, another player said, "Jerry, play your jack." I said, "How do you know I have a jack." He said, "The whole town knows you have a jack, play it!"

A/AD: *What helps prepare people with AS for these types of social encounters?*

Jerry: They need special coaching at a much earlier age. Some of that can come from professionals. If they can have a support group of peers with different challenges, they can trade what they know and maybe even make an initial friend in that group. It gets a lot harder when you deal with adults who were in segregated, abusive settings.

I can't stress enough how important it is to get our people started early in the social area.

Mary: I've already said it. It's hair, makeup, clothes and learning about other people's interests. You can do all of that in your way but if you wear your condition on your sleeve, it won't help at all. Besides, a lot more women have traits like me than you think, without a label. Most of me is as normal as most people. It's the other 5% you stim on.

A/AD: *Do you believe there is an autism culture that has its own set of rules?*

Jerry: Yes, but I think it's overdone. My peer support group has a unique comfort zone and social rules of its own but that's .5 percent of the time, three hours a month. It is too bad it isn't longer and sometimes, I wonder what an autie commune, trading and co-mingling with its surroundings as necessary, would be like.

There's much to be said for having a few hours a month where you walk into a room and you don't have to apologize for being who you are because everybody else there shares your AS.

So, yes, there's definitely an autism culture--people who know exactly what they want to know and when they want to know it.   And they don't settle for less.   You should have been there when Margaret Bauman spoke to an AGUA meeting. Some of us had questions to fire away like arrows in a quiver. Did we ever wear her out!

Mary: I'm very detached from the autistic culture.   I focus on being like normal people so I can make it in the world.   I consider it to be personal growth. I find happiness and achievement in it. I follow normal people's rules. When in Rome, do as the Romans.   It means daily compromise but I am still autistic when I really need to be.   In that sense, I put on a "work-face" like the normals do, too.

I am happy, have a job and go to school to get a better job. Autism is never an excuse that others must accept. I only mention autism when I have done something praise-worthy.

A/AD: *Do you think that people with AS use their lack of social skills as a crutch in a relationship, so they don't have to work as hard as may be needed?*

Jerry: Way too often.

Many peers say, "This is the way I am, I can't change it

because of my condition." They seem to believe because they have AS or autism, everything about them is cast in stone. It's very self-defeating to have that attitude. The autism community track record, in marriages, is even worse than the norm and rigidity is a big reason for that.

There are certainly limits to how much accommodation you can make. But in my AS community, I see too much rigidity, too much insistence on, "Oh, why doesn't the rest of the world just lighten up?" Well, guess what? We're in the minority. 99.8 percent of the world is not going to totally change to suit .2 percent that is afraid to. Compromise is needed.

There are a lot of things about me that I would change, but I know that there are parts about having this condition that I really like and that really helped me. Just like everybody else, I make a lot of compromises. Maybe I don't want to get up four or five times a week, go out and make a living, but I do it. There are lots of things I don't really feel like doing but I do. On the other hand when I have free time to stare at the birds for hours, watch our sunflowers grow and record it, or do any of the other things that really are still classic AS behaviors, I still do those things. But I don't insist on being that person all the time, everywhere.

Temple Grandin can't just flip out every time something bothers her at a conference. I'm sure there are things that go on at any conference that drive her up the wall in a sensory way. She doesn't do it. I don't care who you are, you have to have self-discipline. I think you have to see the big picture.

If you really want your life to be something, you've got to make some kind of peace with the rest of this world so that you can live enough of life the way you really want to live it.

I'll tell you, some people I know in my community are not going to like my book because I'm urging people to take responsibility for their lives and stop using their condition as an excuse. It may be harder but it is not impossible, and this is the only life I get.

Mary: You can't focus on deficits. It's like being an athlete. Refuse limitations. Meet or exceed every goal. Always say, "Yes, I can!" Social skills can be learned. Observe normal people. Incorporate behavior. Still be yourself but also like them. Consider it growth.

A/AD: *And do you think that's part of what prevents them from forming relationships?*

Jerry: Sure it is. It's that rigidity, that absolute insistence on the world following their rules all the time. I've "known" some people through the Internet and I've met some of them at conferences. Most of them are educated, talented adults who are full of anger. They feel absolutely no obligation to control it. It makes them totally unemployable. They have no control over their lives, but they insist that's the way it has to be and they're perfectly justified in their reasoning. That is a sad waste of a lot of lives.

A/AD: *Do people with AS understand how their behaviors affect other people?*

Jerry: I think they do some of the time; I know I do. But I still say things and don't realize the social impact on the audience. We may not get it when we say something but might, after we think about it. Or maybe somebody points it out to us, that what we said ruffled his feathers. I think a lot of us have reached that point. I don't think that Theory of Mind is beyond our reach. I don't think it's a high priority for us.

We're born in a world in which we are constantly fighting to stay afloat and survive. There's not a lot of peace. I think when you're in that kind of world, certain things that normally might be a part of your thinking, like other peoples' perceptions, don't get onto the screen very often. Too many other things crowd it out. It's like you're an air traffic controller and there's just too many planes on the screen. The Theory of Mind plane won't fly until you have those other planes landed.

A/AD: *In your relationships with people, have you learned how to say you're sorry?*

Jerry: Sometimes people tell me, "Stop saying you're sorry. Just don't do it anymore."

I don't think the problem is learning to say you're sorry. The problem is the social learning curve, not being fast or steep enough to suit most people. It was that way in the workplace. It took me a long time to understand that my supervisors didn't have nearly as much time to spend with me as I wanted them to have.

A/AD: *As we close this chapter, what advice would you offer to other people with AS to maximize their success in relationships?*

Jerry: You've got to accept the fact that in certain ways you're always going to be fundamentally different than a lot of other people. Just accept it. Stop fighting it. It's just that way. But on the other hand, you have to keep yourself open to finding ways to negotiate through this world and arrive at a compromise between the way you'd like to be and the way that your workplace or your friends or whatever relationship you want, requires of you.

You have to have some flexibility. You have to forgive yourself for not being normal. There are a lot of well-meaning people around you who think that the only way you could possibly be happy is to become normal. You're never going to be that. You have to take stock of your strengths and your weaknesses and make the most of them. You don't have to be normal. You have to be the best available version of you.

Mary: Love your differences. You are unique. Always be interested in their interests. Tell yourself you can grow. Become a loveable person. There are some people who like people with differences. Once you find someone, try to grow to include him in your world.

A/AD: *Do you feel your AS has removed choices from your life?*

Jerry: I have different choices. AS people are not usually good managers. On the other hand, we are people who do one part of a big project very, very well and very reliably. There might be a Michelangelo in back of us, deciding how this mural is going to be painted and he tells me that I'm going to paint the whale. Whales are my passion and I would probably produce a great whale. But I won't coordinate that whole mural. That's not me. There's a lot more room in the world for good worker ants than queens.

Many of my peers and most people with disabilities feel differently than I do. I have never felt that AS was a disability, even when I lacked a name for it. I just think I am able and incompetent in a skewed, very different way. But I am not disabled. Nobody ever told me I was. I know too many people with more severe levels of autism and with tougher, obvious disabilities, to think of myself in that light.

Mary: I've certainly had a hard time, but I keep going. Right now, AS doesn't impede me. I'm popular at work and in school. My identity is as someone who works hard and has a sense of humor. At cosmetology school, I am nice to everyone and do well, learning hair, nails and facials. I have lots of options and a bright future.

Millennium Films presents ...

They don't fit in. Except together.

mozart & the whale

josh
hartnett

radha
mitchell

mozart & the whale

"Imagination is more important than knowledge."

--Albert Einstein

A dramatic, romantic comedy, *Mozart and the Whale* is inspired by the lives of two people with Asperger's Syndrome, a form of autism, whose emotional dysfunctions threaten to sabotage their budding romance. **Donald** (Josh Hartnett) is a good-natured but hapless taxi driver with a love for birds and a superhuman knack for numbers. Like many AS sufferers, he likes patterns and routines. But when the beautiful but complicated **Isabelle** (Radha Mitchell) joins the autism support group he leads, his life - and his heart - is turned upside down.

The screenplay was written by Academy Award winner Ron Bass and directed by award-winning director Petter Naess. Executive producers are Andreas Thiesmeyer, Josef Lautenschlager, Avi Lerner, Danny Dimbort and Trevor Short. Producers are Robert Lawrence, Frank DeMartini and James Acheson. The creative team includes director of photography Svein Kroevel, editor Miklos Wright, production designer Gary Steele and costume designer Ha Nguyen.

This film is an Equity Pictures Mediafonds/Robert Lawrence production in association with Millennium Films and Swingin' Productions, Inc. starring Josh Hartnett, Radha Mitchell, Gary Cole, Allen Evangelista, Sheila Kelley, Erica Leerhsen, John Carroll Lynch, Nate Mooney, and Robert Wisdom.

mozart & the whale

Josh Hartnett

One of Hollywood's hottest young actors whose ability to transform himself into many interesting forms continues to surprise his audiences.

In 2003 he starred opposite Harrison Ford in *Hollywood Homicide,* and in 2002 he starred in Miramax's *40 Days and 40 Nights.* His comedic performance earned him the ShoWest 2002 Male Star of Tomorrow Award. In 2001, he starred in Ridley Scott's *Black Hawk Down* for Sony Pictures,which re-teamed Josh with producer Jerry Bruckheimer. The film, which is based on Mark Bowden's 1999 nonfiction novel of the same name, told the story of an ill-fated U.S. Humanitarian mission in Somalia which took place on October 3, 1993. Also that year, Hartnett starred in the Jerry Bruckheimer-produced Disney blockbuster *Pearl Harbor* which earned over $1 billion worldwide.

Josh played his first antagonist in the Lions Gate Film *O.* He had the opportunity to play the dark and dangerous character *Hugo* and received critical praise for his work.

In 1999, Josh starred opposite Kirsten Dunst in the critically acclaimed black comedy *The Virgin Suicides*, which was Sofia Coppola's directorial debut. This film was produced by Francis Ford Coppola for American Zoetrope.

Josh made his feature film debut in 1998, co-starring with Jamie Lee Curtis in *Halloween: H20*, for which he was honored with an MTV Movie Award nomination for Best Breakthrough Performance. Also in 1998, he starred in another Miramax project *The Faculty*, directed by Robert Rodriguez.

In the fall of 2004, Josh will be seen in MGM's *Wicker Park* for director Paul McGuigan. Hartnett is currently filming **Mozart and the Whale** written by Ron Bass, a love story between two people (Hartnett and Mitchell) with Asperger's Syndrome, a form of autism, whose emotional dysfunctions threaten to sabotage their budding romance.

In the summer of 2004 he begins filming *The Black Dahlia* for director Brian DePalma.

mozart & the whale

Radha Mitchell

She's building a career as one of Hollywood's newest leading ladies with an upcoming Woody Allen film and roles opposite Denzel Washington, Will Ferrell and Johnny Depp. Mitchell is best known for her performances in *Phone Booth* opposite Colin Farrell, *Pitch Black* with Vin Diesel and *High Art*.

Mitchell has the starring role in the Regency Enterprises/Fox 2000 production *Man on Fire* opposite Denzel Washington where she plays the mother of a missing child who has been kidnapped. A former marine (Washington) devotes himself to avenging her death. She also stars in the upcoming Miramax film *Neverland* with Johnny Depp, Kate Winslet and Dustin Hoffman for director Marc Forster (*Monster's Ball*) with whom she worked in 2000 when she starred and produced the Independent Spirit Award-nominated film *Everything Put Together*.

Mitchell plays the title character in Woody Allen's new Fox Searchlight film *Melinda and Melinda*, opposite Will Ferrell.

Most recently, she starred opposite Colin Farrell in Joel Shumacher's *Phone Booth*. Mitchell starred in the box-office hit *Pitch Black* opposite Vin Diesel. The actress gave a memorable performance as Syd, the young editorial assistant who falls in love with Ally Sheedy's heroin-addicted photographer character in Lisa Cholodenko's critically-acclaimed drama *High Art*. Her role in Emma-Kate Croghan's romantic comedy *Love and Other Catastrophes* was highly praised at both the Cannes and Sundance film festivals.

Other recent film credits include *When Strangers Appear* with Josh Lucas, the independent feature *Dead Heat* opposite Kiefer Sutherland and Anthony LaPaglia, *Nobody's Baby* with Gary Oldman and Skeet Ulrich, and Rodrigo Garcia's *Ten Tiny Love Stories*. On television, she starred with Hank Azaria and Donald Sutherland in NBC's critically-acclaimed mini-series *Uprising* for director Jon Avnet.

Born and raised in Melbourne, Australia, Mitchell began her career acting in Australian television and film while still in high school.

CPSIA information can be obtained at www.ICGtesting.com
Printed in the USA
BVOW07s1123060813

327966BV00002B/174/A